"Filled with truth _____ ern Christians to r_____ _____ __ __ ____ ___ requires of us. A justice-oriented faith will be costly, Joash Thomas warns, but this is not a dour book. Theologically grounded and refreshingly practical, it is above all a compassionate call for all Christians to walk together in the way of Christ."

—**Kristin Kobes Du Mez**, *New York Times* bestselling author of *Jesus and John Wayne*

"Joash Thomas is a gift to the world, and so is this book. With the perfect combination of prophetic fire and pastoral care, Joash reminds us that Jesus and justice go together like blades of scissors or like paddles on a rowboat—or like dal on rice. Joash reminds us that the gospel of Jesus is always good news to the poor and the oppressed, which also explains why it is so often disruptive and offensive to the rich and powerful. But, in the end, the gospel is big enough for everyone, because we have a God who wants to set both the oppressed and the oppressors free. I'm so glad Joash loves the church enough to critique it. Pass this book on to everyone you know."

—**Shane Claiborne**, author, activist, and cofounder of Red Letter Christians

"Hospitable yet bold, this book reimagines a future for the church that prioritizes justice in the way of Jesus. Joash's deep love for the church shines from every page as he invites us all into the group project of liberation."

—**Sarah Bessey**, editor of the *New York Times* bestseller *A Rhythm of Prayer*; author of *Field Notes for the Wilderness: Practices for an Evolving Faith*

"Pastorally disruptive and brilliantly convicting, *The Justice of Jesus* shows how colonization has distorted the gospel of Jesus and harmed the body and soul of the church. Thomas challenges us to rethink the motivations behind our theology, the privileged hierarchies behind our praxis, and to relearn what it means to seek justice, love mercy, and walk humbly with our God. This book can change the church if we will let it."

—**Beth Allison Barr**, professor, Baylor University; *New York Times* bestselling author of *Becoming the Pastor's Wife: How Marriage Replaced Ordination as a Woman's Path to Ministry*

"Joash Thomas deftly exposes the dim colonial frameworks that have long shadowed our theology, flinging open the windows of Scripture to flood us with ancient wisdom and the liberating breath of the Spirit. This work is no mere critique but an invitation to participate in the liberating work and witness of Jesus, the living stream of justice for which our souls have ached. A timely and courageous gift to the global church, this book will leave you grateful for its depth, clarity, and uncompromising authenticity."

—**Danielle Strickland**, author, speaker, and advocate

THE
JUSTICE
OF
JESUS

THE JUSTICE OF JESUS

REIMAGINING YOUR CHURCH'S LIFE TOGETHER
TO PURSUE LIBERATION AND WHOLENESS

JOASH P. THOMAS

BrazosPress
a division of Baker Publishing Group
Grand Rapids, Michigan

© 2025 by Joash P. Thomas

Published by Brazos Press
a division of Baker Publishing Group
Grand Rapids, Michigan
BrazosPress.com

Printed in the United States of America

All rights reserved. No part of this publication may be reproduced, stored in a retrieval system, or transmitted in any form or by any means—for example, electronic, photocopy, recording—without the prior written permission of the publisher. The only exception is brief quotations in printed reviews.

Library of Congress Cataloging-in-Publication Data
Names: Thomas, Joash P., 1993– author.
Title: The justice of Jesus : reimagining your church's life together to pursue liberation and wholeness / Joash P. Thomas.
Description: Grand Rapids, Michigan : Brazos Press, a division of Baker Publishing Group, [2025] | Includes bibliographical references.
Identifiers: LCCN 2025005511 | ISBN 9781587436666 (paperback) | ISBN 9781587436864 (casebound) | ISBN 9781493452194 (ebook)
Subjects: LCSH: Justice—Religious aspects—Christianity. | Liberation theology.
Classification: LCC BR115.J8 T456 2025 | DDC 241/.622—dc23/eng/20250312
LC record available at https://lccn.loc.gov/2025005511

Unless otherwise indicated, Scripture quotations are from the New Revised Standard Version Updated Edition (NRSVue). Copyright © 2021 National Council of Churches of Christ in the United States of America. Used by permission. All rights reserved worldwide.

Scripture quotations labeled NIV are from the Holy Bible, New International Version®, NIV®. Copyright © 1973, 1978, 1984, 2011 by Biblica, Inc.® Used by permission of Zondervan. All rights reserved worldwide. www.zondervan.com. The "NIV" and "New International Version" are trademarks registered in the United States Patent and Trademark Office by Biblica, Inc.®

Portions of this book record the author's present recollection of past events. Dialogue of previous conversations has been re-created and represents the author's accounting of the circumstances in view and not the exact wording of the exchange.

Cover design by Darren Welch Design

Published in association with The Bindery Agency, www.TheBinderyAgency.com.

Baker Publishing Group publications use paper produced from sustainable forestry practices and postconsumer waste whenever possible.

25 26 27 28 29 30 31   7 6 5 4 3 2 1

To my parents, Praveen and Susan Thomas,
for passing down the rich,
ancient Christian faith you inherited
and showing me the way of Jesus by sacrificing so much.
This book only exists because of your faithfulness.

CONTENTS

Introduction 11

Part 1 Cheap Justice Versus the Justice of Jesus

1. Why Justice Seems Antithetical to the Western Church 21
2. The Cost of Just Discipleship 41
3. How Churches Today Are Prioritizing Justice 63

Part 2 Decolonizing the Western Church

4. Decolonizing Our Theology 81
5. Decolonizing Our Communities 97
6. Decolonizing Our Budgets 117

Part 3 How Your Local Church Can Prioritize the Justice of Jesus

7. Prayer 135
8. Advocacy 151
9. Partnership 167

Afterword 181
Acknowledgments 185
Notes 187

INTRODUCTION

"This social justice stuff isn't Christian; it's Marxist."

A friend from church left this comment when I shared online about the work of a Christian human rights organization—one I someday hoped to work for. It rattled me. I was a new immigrant to the United States, and here was a white brother I worshiped alongside saying that my faith-fueled calling to pursue justice was not Christian at all.

What if I'm wrong about this? I remember asking myself. *What if he is right? He is an American Christian, after all.*

It would take me years to unpack the layers of complexity here. Years of following Jesus into the work of systemic justice. Years of studying theology at a leading evangelical seminary. Years of examining the complex history of injustice, sugarcoated with gospel language, in the North American church. Years of working out how Global South Christians allow our theology of justice to be colonized by the Western theological tradition.

I realized over time that this beloved friend was merely the product of his Western church environment. After being challenged in similar ways by other Western Christians in my years of mobilizing churches in Canada and the United States to seek systemic justice, my curiosity was sparked. I began to ask and explore these questions:

- Why do so many Western Christians see the work of systemic justice as separate and distinct from the gospel?
- Why do I, as a Global South Christian, see the work of justice so differently from my Western (and mostly white) siblings?
- Who is ultimately in the right here? Whose vision of justice is more aligned with how Jesus defined it in his gospel?
- Why does any of this matter?

This book is my attempt at providing answers after years of theologically and spiritually wrestling with these questions—all while doing the work of justice with a global community of Christians seeking systemic justice Jesus's way on behalf of millions of vulnerable women, children, and families.

Although I spent my early career as a US political consultant and lobbyist helping my clients hone their public voices, it took me years to find my own voice. Even when I started to deepen my justice theology in seminary and found that I had something to say, it didn't always feel like my voice was my own. Perhaps this was because, at that point, almost all of my theological influences were white American men. That's why, when I first started teaching on justice from Scripture at churches across North America, I probably sounded like most other white American Bible scholars.

Now, there's nothing inherently wrong with learning theology from white American men; some of my favorite authors and teachers of Jesus are white American men. There is, however, something dangerous about learning theology *only* from one segment of the global church. The one holy, catholic, and apostolic church is made up of more than white American men, yet these are the voices that dominate Christian academia and Christian publishing today.

Over time, ministry friends and colleagues began to challenge me to bring out my unique perspectives as a Brown South Asian immigrant. And once I stopped checking my Global South perspective at the door of the Western church, everything began to change.

What do I mean when I say "the Global South" church? I'm referring to the church in the southern hemisphere that operates in contexts with a majority of the world's population. A good portion of these churches operate in postcolonial contexts, but many of these regions, such as Ethiopia, Egypt, and India, have churches that trace their roots back to the first century AD. My own southern Indian family traces its faith back to the apostle Thomas, who is believed to have brought the just and liberating gospel of Jesus of Nazareth to my ancestors in AD 52. Think about it this way: Some of our ancestors were worshiping Jesus in the same era when many white Europeans were still worshiping pagan gods like Thor.

What do I mean when I refer to the "Western" church? I'm referring to the historical, majority-white church in Europe, the United States, and Canada. For the sake of clarity, I am deliberately not lumping the Black church, the diaspora immigrant church, or the Indigenous church into my definition of the Western church. Here's why: These church communities (apart from the diaspora immigrant church to a certain degree) were largely excluded by the Western church. The Black church and the Indigenous church, in fact, were systemically excluded by much of white Western Christianity. So instead of erasing and appropriating their unique identities by lumping them into the Western church, I refer to these Christians as "marginalized Christians," ones Western Christians have much to learn from.

And finally, what do I mean when I say "the gospel"? I mean the just and liberating good news of Jesus of Nazareth as he describes it in Luke 4:18: good news for the poor, freedom for the prisoners, and recovery of sight for the blind "to set free those who are oppressed." Too often, Western Christians narrow down Jesus's gospel to a hyper-spiritual, soul-salvation, punch-your-ticket-to-heaven good news that ignores people crying out for physical liberation, when Jesus's gospel is in truth both spiritual *and* physical. Too often, Western Christians also narrow Jesus's gospel to the doctrines of justification (being redeemed by Christ) and sanctification (becoming more like Christ), while underemphasizing glorification (being made new with Christ when Jesus returns to make all things new). This book is an attempt to broaden Western Christians' understanding of the just and liberating gospel of Jesus—a gospel that has always been good news for our neighbors in poverty and oppression.

My journey of deconstructing my narrow Christian faith and disentangling it from its Western influences led to decolonization. Decolonization led to liberation theology, a theology I acquired from faithful Black and Latino Christians who have historically dealt with great injustice and oppression (whether via systemic racism in the United States or via colonization in the Global South). I also discovered the Latin American Evangelical Left's *Misión Integral* along the way, a theology of US-trained theologians operating in Latin America who quickly realized that their theological constructs were not beneficial in their complex contexts. This is something I deeply resonate with as someone who earned two master's degrees from a leading Western evangelical seminary while also serving with one of the world's largest Christian human rights organizations.

Working for nearly seven years in Western evangelical circles while doing the work of justice has been eye-opening, but it has also given me grace to understand why so many well-intentioned Western Christians have been skeptical that justice is an integral part of the gospel of Christ. Even at the height of the racial awakening of 2020, my white male theological heroes had nothing of significance to offer to a North American society and culture wrestling with questions of justice and injustice. Instead, many of them expressed defensiveness and even hostility. And I couldn't blame them for this because, as white American evangelical men, their personal experience of Christ amid injustice and oppression on the margins was limited.

The reality is that all of us have inherited our faith from imperfect people. This is in fact a beautiful thing. But it's also a really complex thing to reckon with. Just as many white Western Christian ancestors had their blind spots (including their support of colonization and slavery), my St. Thomas Indian Christian ancestors had blind spots too—their participation and complicity in the oppressive caste system, for example. Every pocket of the global church has blind spots. This means we all need each other's eyes to see more clearly so that we can be faithful in the present.

So I took it upon myself to learn. I began to research and write from a theological perspective I had been longing to hear from my heroes and mentors, perspectives on justice and systemic injustice that I could uniquely offer given my professional and lived experiences. As it turns out, I was not the only one longing to challenge and be challenged by the gospel as I knew it. Church leaders, ministry directors, and publishers across North America began to reach out to me, eager to engage with the people in their midst who deeply cared about justice.

What motivated me to partner with Brazos Press for this project (my first book project) was their invitation for me to write in a way that leans toward a hopeful prognosis. Most of us realize that things are broken. Some of us have started to see why things are broken—specifically, the ways in which the

Western church's historical support for colonization has shaped us to resist justice. But very few of us have a sense of how to decolonize our faith and foster a more just future for everyone. As I recently said at a speaking engagement in the Netherlands to a European Christian audience that is faithfully wrestling with the ways in which they have benefited from colonization, *we cannot change the past, but we can be faithful in the present.*

The Justice of Jesus is the book I deeply needed in those early days of deconstructing and decolonizing my theology. This book sheds some light on how we got to this present moment, but it also attempts to do the difficult work of casting a positive vision for what a decolonized, Jesus-centered way of prioritizing justice for our poor and oppressed neighbors looks like on the ground.

This book is divided into three parts. In part 1, I write about justice and the Western church—particularly focusing on why Western Christians in a postcolonial world with colonized theological frameworks naturally resist connecting the work of justice and their Christian faith. I also juxtapose this with hopeful examples of churches across the world today (including North America) that prioritize justice Jesus's way.

In part 2, I offer a few thoughts on decolonizing the local church, specifically through our theology, our posture, and our budgets. In this too I try to cast a positive vision for the Western church by offering examples of churches living out the decolonized, just, and liberating gospel of Christ in our world—both in the past and in the present.

In part 3, I write about how individuals and local churches can prioritize the work of systemic justice through prayer, advocacy, and partnership. While I hope the entirety of this book casts a positive vision of what prioritizing systemic justice can look like for your church, this section is the most practical. My hope is that on completing this book you'll walk away with practices and ideas to help your faith community prioritize justice work that flows from your hope in Jesus. And if you struggle with focus as I do (thank you, neurodivergence!), I hope you feel free to skip around and engage with the sections of this book you feel the most need to engage with on any particular day.

As you read, you may find I've communicated something that makes you uneasy. As I've already mentioned, I'm a Global South Christian seeking a decolonized practice of Christianity that is informed by traditions like those of my St. Thomas Indian ancestors. I've come to realize that if my readers and listeners hear my voice and read my words and come away thinking I sound exactly like a white American evangelical theologian or Bible scholar teaching on justice, then I'll have failed at my task.

This is why if you're a Global South Christian (even a South Asian Christian like myself) who has learned about Christianity primarily from white male American authors and theologians, you'll find that my voice sounds different from the voices you've likely learned from. Reading my perspectives may be uncomfortable for this reason. I want to encourage you to lean in with me in experiencing Jesus in a fresh way—from decolonized and marginalized perspectives.

A Southern Baptist pastor, theologian, and friend once said to me after hearing me teach, "You have a unique way of poking holes in our neatly packaged Western evangelical theological frameworks."

That's what I hope to do with this book.

Finally, everything I share in this book is personal and not a reflection of any past or present employer's public positions.

PART 1

CHEAP JUSTICE VERSUS THE JUSTICE OF JESUS

1

Why Justice Seems Antithetical to the Western Church

> Those who love their neighbor as themselves possess nothing more than their neighbor; yet surely, you seem to have great possessions! How else can this be, but that you have preferred your own enjoyment to the consolation of the many? For the more you abound in wealth, the more you lack in love.
>
> —St. Basil the Great, *On Social Justice*

"What do you mean by 'justice'?"

This is a question I frequently am asked when I talk about justice in my preaching or writing. If you're a Christian advocate for justice, you likely are asked this question quite often as well.

Now perhaps you, if you are a majority-culture Western Christian, see a question like this and think, *Oh, it's probably just a well-intentioned question from someone who does not have a clear understanding of what justice is.*

That's fair. But as someone born and raised in the Global South evangelical church, in which the pursuit of justice is largely normative, whenever I see Christians posing questions like this, I think, *Shouldn't we as Christians be the first to jump out of our seats when we hear of anyone in need of justice? Why this resistance to something that is so close to the heart of God and the gospel of Jesus Christ?*

"What do you mean by 'justice'?"

Interestingly, I've never been asked this question by a non-Christian friend. I've never been asked this question by a Hindu, Muslim, Sikh, Buddhist, or atheist. Come to think of it, I've been asked this question exclusively by well-meaning Western Christians.

There are many ways to answer this question. Back when I first started mobilizing North American churches to prioritize justice, I would try to answer by referencing a Christian definition of justice commonly attributed to church father Augustine of Hippo: "Justice is giving to each person their due." I think this is a terrific Christian framing of justice. This is how I define justice for us in this book too.

But when I share this definition at speaking engagements and continue to get blank stares, I usually go on to elaborate: "Justice is giving to each person the good things that God intended for them. For the survivor of violence, that's healing and restoration. And for the perpetrator of violence, that's accountability for the purpose of restoration."

I've found this to be a particularly helpful way of defining justice for Western evangelical audiences (especially majority-white audiences) that often find their views of justice shaped by their favorite political commentators outside the church. In many of those spaces, and despite the historical Christian teachings on the matter, justice is a bogeyman.

An example of this suspicion of the work of social justice can be found in a 2023 YouTube video titled "Message to the Christian Churches," where best-selling author and psychologist-turned-cultural-commentator (and fellow Canadian) Jordan Peterson says, "You are churches for God's sake. Stop fighting for social justice. Quit saving the bloody planet. Attend to some souls. That's what you're supposed to do. That's your holy duty. Do it. Now. Before it's too late. The hour is nigh."[1]

Political commentators like Peterson have a massive influence on American Christians. In fact, the pastor of an Egyptian Presbyterian church in North America recently lamented to me that the youth at his church are more influenced by Jordan Peterson than they are by fellow Presbyterian Tim Keller. Many of us who engage the Western church in the work of justice often find ourselves running into church leaders or church members with similar sentiments—visions for the church that oppose the just and liberating gospel of Jesus of Nazareth.

Truth be told, these concerns about justice didn't bother me at first. But five years into doing this work of mobilizing the North American church to prioritize justice, I started to notice a holy disillusionment settling into my bones. *Why is it that only people in the church are asking me this question?* And as someone who spent his childhood in the Global South church, *Why am I only being asked this question by Christians in the West?*

If you're a North American Christian with a passion for justice, you've probably faced questions like this. Perhaps you've become numb to statements like the following:

"Define justice."

"Social justice is not biblical justice."

"Justice this world's way is different from justice Jesus's way."

Now to be fair, there *is* a difference between justice Jesus's way and justice the world's way, though not in the ways you've likely been taught. Still, I'm trying to get to a couple of deeper questions here. Where does this resistance to justice movements inside and outside the church come from? And two thousand years after Jesus told us who our neighbor is—the answer being anyone in need of mercy and material liberation, as he taught in the parable of the good Samaritan—why is so much of the Western church still having this conversation?

Like so many others, it took me a long time to realize a deeper truth: *Justice is not the natural disposition of the contemporary Western church.* Martin Luther King Jr. once said, "The arc of the moral universe is long, but it bends toward justice."[2] While I believe this to be true because of God's goodness, I also believe that for centuries now the arc of the Western church has bent in a different direction.

If that sounds harsh, just ask our Black neighbors, many of whose ancestors endured slavery, lynchings, and Jim Crow segregation, all of which were widely embraced and given theological cover by Christians. Just ask our Indigenous neighbors, whose ancestors were victimized by genocide, erasure, and church-run residential schools. Or ask my ancestors, whose land, culture, and way of relating to God were for centuries usurped by colonial Western powers backed by the Catholic, Dutch Reformed, and Anglican churches. Because of my own privilege as a male, upper-middle-class immigrant from the Global South, it took me until 2020 to fully realize the Western church has a history of repeatedly failing our poor and oppressed neighbors.

Many North American Christians' responses to events and movements like Black Lives Matter, the violent transition of political power in the United States, and the COVID-19 pandemic were a rude awakening to many of us who have hungered for righteousness and justice in the church. It revealed to us a simple yet poignant truth: Instead of being shaped by the liberating Spirit of God that anointed Jesus to bring good news to people in poverty and oppression (Luke 4:18), much of the Western church was shaped by a theology that prioritizes the salvation of souls at the cost of the dignity and liberation of human bodies.

We need to unpack this theology in order to understand why justice remains a stumbling block for many Christians in the West.

"What Do You Mean by 'Decolonization'?"

"Decolonization" is a word that gets thrown around a lot these days. It's an aspirational value for many outside the church, such as the international development community I often rub shoulders with in my work. When I speak about decolonization to Christian audiences internationally, I've noticed a trend. On a scale of "most comfortable" to "least comfortable," for the most part, European Christian audiences I've spoken to are most comfortable with the word. American audiences seem to be the least comfortable with it. Canadian audiences seem to be somewhere in between.

The work of decolonization will always be a threat to the beneficiaries of colonization, especially those who have not wrestled much with how they have benefited from colonization. Still, we can't really understand the *why* of working for decolonization without coming to terms with the darkness of Western colonization.

Here's how Duke University professor Walter Mignolo defines colonization, or colonialism: "Colonialism is a practice of domination, which involves the subjugation of one people by another."[3] One could argue that colonization has always been around. Nevertheless, the system of modern colonization that has shaped much of today's postcolonial world began in the fifteenth and sixteenth centuries with Europe's military subjugation of the Global South. Western colonization occurred where European countries used military might to systematically extract persons (for slavery) and resources from other people and locales. Colonization created racial hierarchies based on external characteristics. In fact, many historians argue that it's impossible to understand or dismantle racism without understanding that colonization is the system that entrenched and enabled racism.

While European colonization officially ended in the mid-twentieth century, its aftereffects remain in the forms of extreme poverty, global hunger, racial hierarchies, and conflict in many liberated former colonies (including the terrorism and genocide taking place in the Israel-Palestine region at the time of this book's writing).[4]

As someone born and raised in a country that threw out its colonial oppressors less than a century ago (in 1947), I can confidently state that colonization isn't a mere academic concept or ideological talking point. My family has lived and somehow survived the effects of colonization firsthand.

Colonization's shameful effects are by no means a distant relic of times long past. For example, my grandparents were born while the British still controlled much of India. My great-grandparents spent the vast majority of their lives in colonized India. Queen Elizabeth II, who passed away in 2022, became second in line to the throne while India was still colonized in 1936. Most of Africa was only decolonized from the 1950s to the 1970s, during Elizabeth II's reign as monarch.

Here's something else that might surprise you: The Portuguese were the first to colonize much of Asia (including India). In fact, Portugal's first colony in Asia, established in the year 1510, was the modern-day Indian region of Goa, just a few hours south of where I grew up in Mumbai.

But do you know when the Portuguese officially left India? The answer might astound you: December 1961, the first year of John F. Kennedy's presidency. Even then, the Portuguese refused to leave India willingly, departing only after numerous protests that resulted in the Indian government taking decisive military action.

You might be wondering where the Western church was when Europe was colonizing vast swaths of the globe. The answer is that they were largely on the side of the oppressing colonizers. If you are tempted to blame this on the Catholic Church, keep in mind that the Dutch Reformed Church backed the Dutch East India Company, which colonized much of Asia. Abraham Kuyper, a Dutch Reformed Church leader, is still widely respected today despite his colonizing apologetics.

The Church of England backed the British Empire. In fact, repenting of its support of colonization in recent years, the Church of England has publicly admitted that much of its wealth was built on the backs of people it oppressed through slavery and colonization. And last but not least, Southern Baptists and Southern Presbyterians in the US South aided and abetted colonization with their support of slavery and Jim Crow.

Esteemed Yale theologian Willie James Jennings argues in his book *The Christian Imagination* that the Western Christian tradition has been deeply shaped by a colonial mindset—a mindset that has marginalized and devalued non-European cultures and peoples. He argues that this colonial imagination has influenced how Christians understand God, humanity, and the world in ways that often reinforce systems of power and oppression. Decolonization, in Jennings's view, calls for *a reimagining of Christianity that challenges and transcends the limitations of the colonial imagination.*[5]

This is exactly the type of work I hope we can undertake together over these next chapters: the work of reimagining Christianity by disentangling our faith from its colonial influences so that we can prioritize the justice of Jesus for our marginalized neighbors.

The Colonizer's Gospel

We often forget that *injustice doesn't just hurt people in oppression; it also hurts the oppressor*. We will never be free until we come to terms with this reality.

As a child of colonization, I have no doubt about this: Colonizer theology hurt not only colonized peoples but also colonizers and the Western Christians on their side. And it is hurting their theological and ecclesial descendants today, even if they do not realize this. The colonizer's gospel stands in stark contrast with the just and liberating gospel of Jesus of Nazareth. Here are four key tenets of the colonizer's gospel that we need to examine and counter with the full biblical and historical Christian witness.

Tenet 1: Jesus Came Primarily to Save Souls

Colonizers and slaveholders led colonized and enslaved peoples to believe that Jesus was more concerned about their souls than their bodies. Many eighteenth- and nineteenth-century theologians in the United States explicitly taught enslaved Black people that God desired for them to stay in bondage while wanting them to put their faith in Jesus for spiritual salvation. False man-made doctrines, such as the "curse of Ham," (a concocted teaching that Africans were descendants of Noah's cursed son, Ham) were brandished against Black people in slavery to keep them racially, socially, and economically subjugated.[6]

This is the same theology that undergirds the question that many of us working in the anti-trafficking space often hear from Western church leaders today. After I share stories of children being sexually exploited twenty to thirty times a day, North American church leaders will sometimes ask, "What's the point of rescuing children from sex trafficking if they don't hear the gospel and go to hell?" Reader, as someone who has met dozens of rescued survivors of child trafficking, I feel like I need to take a shower anytime I hear a question like this.

The colonizer's gospel conveniently neglects the truth attested throughout Scripture, that the gospel of Jesus of Nazareth is spiritual *and* physical. After all, as I often say in sermons while teaching from Luke 4:18, if our gospel is not good news for the poor, freedom for the captive, recovery of sight for the blind, and liberation for the oppressed, then our gospel is not the gospel of Jesus Christ.

We know Jesus's gospel was physical because he took the form of human flesh and came down to earth to redeem and restore all of creation (including humankind) from sin (including injustice and oppression). And we know that Jesus's gospel is physical because he rose from the dead and has ensured our physical resurrection from the dead when he returns.

Tenet 2: Justice Is a Worthy Pursuit, but Evangelism and Discipleship Are More Important

It's quite common for advocates like myself to hear statements prioritizing evangelism over social justice from church leaders. This is tragic, because the Jesus of Nazareth we encounter in the Gospels deeply cares about both physical and spiritual liberation. This is why we see Jesus healing people (who desired to be healed), casting out demons, and feeding hungry people throughout the accounts of his life and ministry.

These acts aren't just vivid, spiritual teaching points but a direct expression of God's plan to restore all humans to full flourishing, which necessarily includes physical flourishing. As someone who was himself a marginalized, Brown, Palestinian, Jewish refugee, Jesus of Nazareth engaged in justice, verbal proclamation of the kingdom of God, and discipleship. These are all connected and hence cannot be separated from one another. Additionally, the ability to see justice as separate, less than, or secondary to evangelism and discipleship is a privilege, a privilege that the survivors of violence I advocate for do not have.

Tenet 3: Social Hierarchies Are Natural and Part of God's Design

The colonizer's gospel is built on power, with the racially and economically privileged at the top and everyone else subjugated at the bottom. Think about it: For the colonizers and enslavers to succeed in getting people to neglect the just and liberating gospel of Jesus of Nazareth, they had to argue that God always intended for hierarchical structures to exist both inside and outside the church. According to the proper ordering of things—in their view—white men of means were intended to occupy the top tier, and Black, Brown, and Asian people were relegated to the bottom, with women and children at the very bottom. They deceived both themselves and others by fashioning interpretations that suited their own interests and agendas.

It should not surprise us that the theological and ecclesial descendants of colonizer and slaveholder church leaders frequently push back on justice efforts or use labels like "liberal" or "woke" when faithful, justice-oriented Christians start asking questions about power dynamics that inherently lead to vulnerable people groups being marginalized.

I know many white evangelical pastors who were justice oriented in 2020 but became anti–social justice crusaders as soon as the political winds shifted and 2021 rolled around. Similarly, I know of Christian ministries that did away with their diversity, equity, and inclusion programs in early 2025. Much like the rich young ruler who walked away from Jesus after realizing he couldn't cast aside his great wealth (much of which was likely tied to a privileged status in the Roman Empire[7]), these Christian leaders, it seems to me, also chose to walk away from

Jesus's ways when confronted with the personal cost of giving up their power, comforts, and privileges.

The kingdom of God being ushered in by the Holy Spirit has zero concern for constructed social and authoritative hierarchies. And making way for God's new creation will always mean upsetting the order of things. Or in the words of Paul in Galatians 3:28, "There is no longer Jew or Greek; there is no longer slave or free; there is no longer male and female, for all of you are one in Christ Jesus."

Tenet 4: Unity Demands Uniformity

The colonizer's gospel makes no room for diverse expressions of Christian faith. This is why so many of the inheritors of the colonizer's gospel in North America look down on other (often more ancient) traditions within the faith. These Christians are conditioned to see their way of worshiping Jesus as the only appropriate way of worshiping Jesus.

In his book *Rescuing the Gospel from the Cowboys*, Indigenous theologian Richard Twiss highlights the resistance of many Western Christians (in addition to many Indigenous evangelical pastors) to contextualize and develop Indigenous expressions of the Christian faith because they often look different from the white expressions of Christianity they are accustomed to.[8]

I too have been a part of white Western churches where threats to uniformity were seen as an affront to unity. Many years ago, I was a pastoral intern and church-planting team member at a church within a denomination that was historically founded by leaders who sought to preserve racist theology and structures. As long as I came across as "like-minded" and in line with their theology, I was welcome. But the moment I stepped out of line on non-creedal issues—that is, beliefs that do not conflict with the Apostles' Creed and the Nicene Creed, the earliest creeds of the global church—I was labeled by some as "divisive" and "unqualified" for pastoral leadership, solely because I had a different conviction on a non-creedal matter (in this case, my views on racial justice). Instead of being seen as a brother from a marginalized community to love in a moment of national racial reckoning, I became a problem to be dealt with. This is what the colonizer's gospel does; it demands unity in the form of uniformity and diminishes those who refuse to assimilate by labeling them as "heretical" or "woke."

My experience with this colonizing side of Western Christianity is not unlike the experience of my St. Thomas Christian ancestors in southern India in their first encounter with Western Christians (discussed in more detail in chap. 5). We St. Thomas Christians from India trace our faith ancestry back to the apostle Thomas's missionary efforts in southern India in AD 52. Thomas is believed to have planted seven churches in Kerala before he was martyred in Chennai. This indigenous Christian tradition went on to thrive as a unified, pluralistic, and ecumenical community for centuries with the support of Syrian and Persian churches, despite being in the religious minority in India.

All of that changed in the sixteenth century, when the Portuguese showed up along with Catholic missionaries. These missionaries came with the explicit mandate of subjugating the St. Thomas Church in India to Catholic liturgy and the pope's authority—especially because my St. Thomas ancestors farmed much of the spice-fertile regions that the Portuguese came to conquer. Despite the St. Thomas Indian Church's many efforts to live in harmonious ecumenism with their Portuguese brethren and the Roman Catholic Church (just as they had for centuries with the Syrian Church and the Persian Church, along with their Hindu, Buddhist, and Muslim neighbors), they discovered that their colonizers had no intentions of tolerating, much less embracing, pluralistic and ecumenical values.[9]

By falsely branding all St. Thomas Christians as Nestorian heretics, the Catholic Church attempted to confiscate and ban all of their preserved Byzantine Syriac liturgies, prayer scriptures, and other religious documents. As part of fort to fully consolidate the St. Thomas Indian Church, Portuguese also tried to impose the Roman Catholic teach of celibacy on clergy, making already-married clergy member abandon their spouses and children. Think about that. Portuguese Catholics were so committed to the superiority of their way of worshiping Jesus that they were okay with creating widows and orphans to sustain Christian uniformity that aligned with their preferences. My ancestors ultimately revolted against the Portuguese and reinstated their autonomous church leadership structure with the help of the Syrian Church and the rival Dutch colonial powers.

To the Portuguese colonizers and the Roman Catholic Church of the sixteenth and seventeenth centuries, the mere existence of an autonomous, indigenous Christian tradition tracing its roots all the way back to Christ through St. Thomas was viewed as a threat.[10] And there could be no unity in diversity. The colonizer's gospel demands that their way of worship be given precedential priority.

How the Colonizer's Gospel Harms the Church

Colonizer theology is bad not only for people in oppression but also for the theological and ecclesial descendants of the colonizers. It shouldn't surprise us that droves of people are leaving a Western church that comes across as allergic to any justice movements inside or outside of it.

As my friend Zach Lambert, pastor of Restore Church in Austin, Texas, often says, "The vast majority of people walking away from Christianity in America are not rejecting the person and work of Jesus. They are rejecting faulty biblical interpretations that lead to bigotry, oppression, and marginalization. This rejection isn't unchristian. It is Christlike."[11]

Maybe you resonate with this. Maybe you consider yourself to be a faithful Christian who can no longer in good conscience be a part of a church that neglects justice or treats it as secondary to "more important spiritual matters." Maybe you or people you love are considering walking away from the faith altogether because of the institutional church's complicity in white supremacy, sexism, and Christian nationalism. Or maybe you are somewhere in between, loving Jesus while wrestling with the pain and trauma heaped on the bodies of marginalized peoples by Christ's body, the church.

Wherever you are, as estranged as you may feel by the church, I want you to know that you are not an anomaly from the perspective of the global, historical church. If anything, people like yourself are the norm. We are a chosen people, a royal priesthood, a holy nation, God's special possession even. And it shouldn't surprise us that many of the churches that have inherited the colonizer's gospel are crumbling from within because of a wide range of issues, from sexual abuse crises to misogyny to white supremacy.

Some of these churches may look like they're thriving in the short run. I've known many faithful Canadian church leaders who have lost countless members over the past few years every time the church took a bold stance on justice issues. But in the end, churches that ignore justice will find themselves snuffed out. That's because the colonizer's gospel pales in comparison to the goodness of the just and liberating gospel of Jesus of Nazareth—a gospel that proclaims the arrival of God's kingdom in the here and now. The counterfeit gospel of the colonizers just doesn't hold up when compared to the gospel of Jesus of Nazareth. And the "one holy, catholic, and apostolic church," as the ancient creeds put it, always withstands the test of time and false doctrine.

It's important that we give ourselves permission to be infuriated by the history of colonization and the Western church's historical support of colonization. Unless we are honest about where we have come from, we will never be liberated. Lest we forget, colonization and its enduring effects on our postcolonial world are also infuriating to the heart of God.

If reading about the history of colonization has made you slightly uncomfortable, I want you to put yourself in the shoes of my ancestors. Or the millions of people separated from their homelands who were treated like property in the brutal transatlantic slave trade. Or the millions of people living in generational poverty because colonization decimated their local economies and their health-care, public justice, environment, and sanitation ecosystems.

It is in discomfort that we truly identify with our marginalized and oppressed neighbors. And unless we incarnationally identify with our marginalized and oppressed neighbors like Jesus did, the gospel will never fully be actualized as good news for people in poverty and oppression.

Know That Things *Can* Be Different

What if I told you that things do not have to be this way? What if I told you that our past does not have to determine our future? What if I told you that our future as the Western church could look drastically different from the past? What if I told you that Jesus redeems everything and everyone decimated by sin and its effects?

And what if I told you that the Spirit of God is constantly at work in restoring his people to the perfect image of God that we see embodied in Christ at an individual, collective, and systemic level?

The reason I wrote this book is because I believe that a different future is possible—a future in which, instead of being known for our complicity in injustice, the Western church is known for its humility in repenting of its historical shortcomings, while also being known for cultivating a just and equitable community, where every tear is wiped away, where all oppression shall cease, and where God's vision for shalom is fully restored on earth as it is in heaven.

I believe in this future because I have seen glimpses of it across the global church as well as in pockets of the Western church. Over these next few pages, I want you to join me in dreaming and envisioning this just future together, regardless of where you are in your journey of pursuing Jesus and justice.

Perhaps you're a North American church leader who doesn't need to be convinced that a just, decolonized future is possible for the Western church. You simply find yourself yearning for fresh inspiration to teach and pursue it. I pray that this book provides that for you.

Perhaps you're a Western Christian who is actively involved in your local church and feels the prophetic urge to challenge your community to prioritize justice. I pray that this book is a helpful resource for you to do just that.

Maybe you're a Jesus follower who is completely disillusioned by the ways in which his body, the church, has failed to embody his just ways. You're in desperate need of a positive vision for what it looks like to prioritize justice in the church today. I pray that this book is a healing balm to your body and soul.

Or maybe you're someone who doesn't really identify as a Jesus follower. You may be intrigued by a Brown, two-time immigrant church leader like myself talking about things like justice and decolonization for the Western church. I'm honored you're here and hope this book inspires you to see Jesus and his church in a fresh, new light.

"But Why Focus So Much on the Church?"

I am frequently asked by dear friends who love Jesus but have given up on institutional Christianity why I focus so much on the church. It's a valid question. Maybe you wonder about this matter too, which is why I will address it now before we go further.

First, the primary reason I focus on the church so much is because I deeply love the body of Christ on earth. I make no attempts to hide throughout the book that I am first and foremost a Churchman (meaning I have dedicated my life to the service of the church). And that's "Churchman" with a capital C. I love the global, historical Christian church, despite our historical and present shortcomings. I'm fiercely ecumenical because, as a St. Thomas Indian Christian, over the past two thousand years my southern Indian ancestors have worshiped Jesus in a wide variety of Christian traditions, ranging from Eastern (Syrian) Orthodox to Roman Catholic to Anglican to Brethren to Pentecostal. So ecumenism is very much in my DNA.

Over the past three decades, I have worshiped and experienced Jesus in Pentecostal, Reformed, Southern Baptist, Anglican, and nondenominational contexts in three different countries. I've served Jesus in house churches, small churches, midsize churches, and megachurches. I've been a member of ethnically homogeneous churches, ethnically diverse churches, majority-white churches, and majority-immigrant churches. And I'm deeply grateful for each of these experiences of Jesus and his body.

Because of my love for the whole church, I find myself unable to look down on any one denomination, tradition, or type of church. Similarly, because of my love for the whole church, I find myself unable to hold up any one Christian tradition as the perfect tradition.

At the time of this book's release, I am an ordained deacon in an Anglican convergence denomination actively pursuing ordination as a priest. I am accountable to the fellow clergy in my diocese, including my bishops.

Throughout Christian history, the vast majority of prophetic voices calling for reform have belonged to leaders within the church. Now, this realization is not to dismiss those outside the church calling for reform. Their voices are much needed too. But I want to note right off the bat that everything I say in this book is born of a deep love for the church.

So many prophetic voices have offered truthful, challenging teachings to the church while still being rooted in a deep love for it. Dietrich Bonhoeffer, Martin Luther King Jr., and Desmond Tutu were all church leaders, as were the Latin American liberation theologians who have shaped much of my theology, including Leonardo Boff, Óscar Romero, and Gustavo Gutiérrez, all Catholic clergy.

It is impossible to love the church without being honest about the ways in which we have historically failed to love God and neighbor. And it is even more impossible to love Jesus (the head of the church) without being honest about the ways in which we continue to fail to love God and neighbor.

A New Reality

I'd like you to imagine a new reality with me:

> What if our local churches became closely and widely associated with justice?
> What if our churches were known more for their contribution to the common good than their zeal for simply converting their neighbors and punching their "get-out-of-hell-free" tickets?
> What if our churches became known as local centers for unconditional justice in our communities instead of places people go for immediate help but bounce as soon as they're expected to attend Bible studies?
> What if our Western local churches also were viewed by members of the local community (especially by our

Hindu, Muslim, Jewish, Sikh, and Buddhist neighbors) as trustworthy first points of contact for their local justice needs?

What if our local churches became places where people felt drawn to explore spiritual liberation in Jesus because of the physical liberation they received through the body of Christ?

What if people walked into the doors of our churches eager to experience the just and liberating gospel of Christ being proclaimed in a way that ministers not only to their spiritual needs but also to their physical and emotional needs?

Welcome to the messy, prophetic, repentant, and yet hope-filled work of recovering salt, light, and liberation in the Western church!

REFLECTION QUESTIONS

1. What do you find yourself resonating with in this chapter?
2. What ideas do you find yourself resisting in this chapter? What do you think is motivating that?
3. What do you hope to receive and take away from this book?
4. Have you ever seen justice and physical liberation as a key facet of the gospel of Jesus Christ? Why or why not?

2

The Cost of Just Discipleship

Like anybody, I would like to live a long life—longevity has its place. But I'm not concerned about that now. I just want to do God's will. . . . And so I'm happy tonight. I'm not worried about anything; I'm not fearing any man.

—Martin Luther King Jr.,
in a speech given the night before his murder

If you ever have the opportunity to listen to me preach, you'll likely hear me repeat one thing over and over: *The justice of Jesus is expensive. It will cost you something. In fact, it may even cost you everything.* Before we move forward with casting a positive vision for justice in our churches and Christian communities, I want to acknowledge this uncomfortable fact: Pursuing the justice of Jesus in the world is hard.

Many Western Christians seem to expect that justice work is efficient, exciting, and easy. Perhaps you're picturing scenes from all the movies you've watched featuring US Navy Seals kicking down doors to rescue children from sex trafficking. But Scripture, history, and firsthand experience have taught me that justice Jesus's way is often messy, mundane, and arduous.

Cheap Justice

After George Floyd, Ahmaud Arbery, and Breonna Taylor were killed in 2020, I spoke with many pastors in the US South who wanted to start teaching about justice from a Christian lens in their churches. They asked me for recommended resources and thoughts on how they could teach biblical justice and disciple their people in it.

As a quick aside, I've moved away from the label "biblical justice" because I've come to understand that all justice is God's justice. In a world where the Spirit of God is transcendent and where Christ is supreme, there is no "biblical justice" versus "secular justice." If anything, I believe we use labels like this because they conveniently allow us to refrain from advocating for people and groups we wish to distance ourselves from.

Let me go a step further. The only categories of secular justice that are truly secular (or even in opposition to Christ's justice) are types of justice that include retributive justice, violent justice, and punitive justice—categories of justice that often pass for "biblical" yet fly in the face of how we see Jesus of Nazareth portrayed in the Gospels.

While I concede that the Bible includes many examples of the above categories of justice, and while I am a theologian and not a Bible scholar, one way of faithfully wrestling with these texts is learning to distinguish between what the Bible *prescribes* (what it directs us to do) and what it *describes* (what it gives an accounting of). And since, in the view of Christians, the purpose of Scripture is primarily to point us to Jesus, anything that stands in stark contrast to Jesus's teachings and actions in the Gospels should be examined and, if needed, rejected.

As I spoke with American pastors in 2020 about what it might look like to disciple their churches in justice, I remember feeling greatly encouraged. After all, many of these were church communities I had spent years engaging and getting zero traction with. Perhaps the Spirit of God was doing something unique throughout the North American church based on what I was seeing in the Bible Belt.

Indeed, the Spirit was doing something unique across the church landscape in 2020. In the years since then, I have sat alongside dozens of justice advocates who have told me about their journeys of being awakened to prioritize justice as an active part of their faith. But like these well-intentioned pastors and church leaders in 2020, I too assumed that discipling their church communities in the justice of Jesus would be easy. How naive I was! Time reveals all things.

When 2020 had passed and 2021 rolled around, these pastors started facing resistance and backlash revolving around critical race theory (a legal academic theory that racism is historically embedded in American society and institutions, which many of these pastors were unaware of up until that point). People accustomed to privilege and power in their church communities started to feel threatened because of increased conversations about racial justice for their Black, Brown, and Asian neighbors.

One pastor I know reminded his community to "mourn with those who mourn" in response to George Floyd's murder, and a few families decided to leave his church as a result. This white pastor genuinely wanted to build a multiethnic community at his church. He wanted the minority church members to feel safe in a majority-white church community, and he wanted their Black and Brown neighbors to feel that they would be welcomed there. But the departing families wanted none of it. Even though their pastor was faithfully (and literally) teaching from Romans 12:15, they told him that they were concerned he was advocating for "Marxist ideas" such as racial justice, because justice was viewed as a political agenda rather than a biblical mandate. Eventually, this pastor moved to another church, where he was hesitant to even mention multiethnicity because of all the backlash he faced at his previous church.

Another pastor I know would frequently host guests on his podcast in 2020 to talk about biblical justice. But when 2021 came around, he started developing concerns about critical race theory and being perceived as "woke." He was okay seeking justice as long as he wasn't seen as a Marxist. And he was okay with others in the church seeking justice as long as they weren't moving away from his safe political preferences.

As much as I love these two pastors, it grieves me to say that they are no longer seeking justice Jesus's way. They're seeking justice America's way—ways that don't cost them. While the justice of Jesus requires us to prioritize justice despite personal cost, justice the American Empire's way shapes us to prioritize individual, material success over the self-sacrificing love of Jesus for our marginalized neighbors. And just like the rich young ruler we see in the Gospels, they're unwilling to pursue Jesus in a way that has a cost to them. Dietrich Bonhoeffer calls this "cheap grace" in his book *The Cost of Discipleship*. Bonhoeffer, a German church leader who witnessed the rise of Nazism in Germany (including within the German church), made this astute observation: "Cheap grace is the grace we bestow on ourselves. Cheap grace is the preaching of forgiveness without requiring repentance, baptism without church discipline, communion without confession."[1]

Perhaps what we're seeing in much of the Western church is the pursuit of "cheap justice," which is a shallow, performative pursuit of justice.

- Cheap justice is participating in annual social media campaigns to stand in solidarity with survivors of human trafficking while doing nothing with your money, skills, and advocacy to support local and global anti-trafficking organizations.
- Cheap justice is posting a black square on your social media in solidarity with Black Lives Matter in 2020, then dropping the pursuit of racial justice once the news cycle moves on to other things.
- Cheap justice is claiming to be "pro-life from the womb to the tomb" and then looking the other way when political parties and politicians lock migrant children in cages, separate migrant children from their families, and bus migrant families to other states to score cheap political points.
- Cheap justice is claiming to love your neighbor while supporting elected officials who cut social safety nets and international development aid to families in poverty at home and abroad.

Cheap justice requires nothing of us. Cheap justice is a slap in the face of Jesus and his just gospel. And the body of Christ is called to ceaselessly fight and peacefully resist a kind of justice in word or sentiment alone, a kind of justice that has no net positive impact on our neighbors close or far.

Before we go any further, I want to pause and celebrate something: You made it this far!

I realize that I have probably made you at least slightly uncomfortable by drawing you closer to what is hopelessly broken. But now that we have started to wrestle with what is hopelessly broken, we can finally start to dream of a positive vision for justice Jesus's way together.

The Justice of Jesus

What is the justice of Jesus? And how is it different from the cheap justice that we often see in the Western church? The parable of the good Samaritan (Luke 10:25–37) continues to be an excellent model for what justice Jesus's way looks like.

A traveler from Jerusalem to Jericho is ambushed by a band of thieves and is brutally assaulted and left for dead. Both a priest and a Levite walk by him and refuse to inconvenience themselves for the sake of their neighbor. Instead of stopping to help this man, they pass by him on the other side of the road.

But a Samaritan, a marginalized outsider with questionable theology, comes into contact with the helpless victim. He patches him up and then takes him to an inn where he can heal. He pays the innkeeper two days of his wages and promises to come back to reimburse him for any additional expenses incurred in the care of this stranger, thereby proving to be a better neighbor than the two religious leaders who looked the other way.

In the following sections, we look at four truths we can learn about the justice of Jesus from the example of the Good Samaritan.

The Justice of Jesus Is Radically Inclusive

In the same way that the Good Samaritan shares space with the victim of injustice, justice Jesus's way also shares space with victims of injustice. The Good Samaritan makes an intentional choice to share space with the victim of violence whose path he crosses. More importantly, the justice of Jesus is radically inclusive because this is also what God does for us. What does God do in making himself known to us through Christ? He shares space with us by entering into our suffering and then inviting us to go on mission with him to heal the suffering of this world.

Just like the first two religious travelers who pass by their marginalized neighbor, so many of us are accustomed to being selfish with the gospel entrusted to us. Because of Western individualism, we think our faith is just for us. We make our faith about just us, so much so that when we see earthly suffering and injustice, we try to avoid it by looking the other way. Or we look past the suffering and oppression being inflicted on our neighbors' bodies so that we can keep the focus on their souls. Our individualized salvation-focused gospel has nothing to say to the worst injustices of this world.

But when we live this way, we forget that we have been victims of this broken world too. And we Christians forget that we ourselves were once far away from the grace of God. Furthermore, we forget that if Jesus hadn't entered the picture and shared space with us, we would still be far away from that grace. But the gospel is not about just us. And it's not *for* just us either. The just and liberating gospel of Christ is for all of creation, including those on the fringes of society. And especially those forgotten and abandoned on the side of the road, including those like the nameless man on the Jericho road. We are instructed to count among our neighbors even people who have never been accepted by religions or societies due to their being seen as impure or unclean. If the good news of Jesus is not good news for people who are poor and oppressed, it is not good news for any of us. And Jesus's vision for his gospel is inclusive of *everyone*, even our worst enemies.

The Justice of Jesus Is Holistic

Justice the world's way is shortsighted. It often focuses on instant gratification and quick wins. But the Good Samaritan shows us that justice Jesus's way is holistic. The first thing the Good Samaritan does is to intentionally share space with the victim of injustice. To do this, he humbles himself and draws closer to him. But he doesn't just look on this suffering man and offer thoughts and prayers before moving along. The Good Samaritan gets his hands (and his honor) dirty by tending to the man and bandaging his wounds with oil and wine. After this, he doesn't just leave him where he is. The Good Samaritan puts the injured man on his own donkey and takes him to an inn for further restorative care.

Here's one of my key takeaways from this text, inspired by the interpretations of many church fathers, such as Irenaeus, Origen, Ambrose, and Augustine: Jesus is the Good Samaritan, and the church is the inn.[2] Just as the Good Samaritan entrusts the care of the victim of injustice to the inn, Jesus entrusts the care of people in oppression to the church. And just like the Good Samaritan promises to return and hold the innkeeper accountable, Jesus will also hold the church and its leaders accountable for the way we treat victims of injustice when he returns.

But unlike the Good Samaritan, who can only rescue and restore the victim of injustice, Jesus (the Great Samaritan) can and will do a lot more at his return. He will also repair the broken systems that allow the violence that takes place on the Jericho road. Martin Luther King Jr. says it best: "On the one hand, we are called to play the good Samaritan on life's roadside; but that will be only an initial act. One day we must come to see that the whole Jericho road must be transformed so that men and women will not be constantly beaten and robbed as they make their journey on life's highway. True compassion is more than flinging a coin to a beggar; it is not haphazard and superficial. It comes to see that an edifice which produces beggars needs restructuring."[3]

The Western church has historically been adept at playing the Good Samaritan on life's roadside by rescuing and restoring victims of oppression. We've even arguably mastered the art of flinging the occasional coin to people in poverty. Nevertheless, as Dr. King challenges us, we must become better at addressing the larger systems (such as justice, public health, social services, and education) that allow injustice and oppression to thrive in the first place. If the just and liberating gospel of Jesus is good news to all of creation, it is good news to both broken individuals and broken institutions.

The Justice of Jesus Is Expensive

Justice Jesus's way is not only radically inclusive and holistic; it is also expensive. The justice of Jesus comes at a great personal cost. If seeking justice does not cost us, we are likely not doing what Jesus asks of us. After all, seeking justice cost the Good Samaritan his comfort, his personal vehicle (his donkey), and two days' wages.

In fact, if we're doing things right—as the Old Testament prophets, John the Baptist, Dietrich Bonhoeffer, and Martin Luther King Jr. did—justice Jesus's way might even cost us everything. I'll leave this point for now, because later in this chapter I share specific examples of how the justice of Jesus is costing church communities in the Western church today.

The Justice of Jesus Is Nonviolent

Truth requires no violence. And "truth" that requires violence is no truth. Just as Jesus's gospel is a gospel of peace, Jesus's justice is also a justice of peace. It is a justice of shalom, or wholeness. And just as "truth" that requires violence is no truth, "justice" that requires violence on the part of the church is also no justice.

Jesus displays his preference for peace at the cross of Calvary. If the almighty and all-powerful Jesus chose peace while being unjustly tortured, shamed, and murdered on the cross, and if Jesus will choose to peacefully restore the earth without any violence at his return, Christians must also seek justice in peaceful ways. In a world riddled with violence, Jesus invites us to resist pursuing justice the world's way by laying aside our swords, just as Jesus called Peter to lay aside his sword when Peter wanted to protect Jesus from becoming a victim of injustice (John 18:10–11).

Whenever I talk about the nonviolent ways of Jesus, I am often challenged by Western Christians with Revelation 19:15, where Jesus defeats evil once and for all on his return with a sharp sword coming out of his mouth. Nevertheless, in my research I've found many within the early church and the global church (including many conservative evangelical Bible scholars) who see this language as poetic, with the "sharp sword" referring to a word that comes out of Jesus's mouth to ensure his victory. This prevalent interpretation of Revelation 19:15 is also in line with the peace-loving Jesus we see throughout the Gospels. Think about it. The same Jesus who spoke the universe into existence with his words (along with the other persons of the triune God) is perfectly able to defeat evil on his return with a single word—without any need for violence.

Now, I am not saying that there is not a place for the use of the sword on the part of the state to protect vulnerable, oppressed people. To argue for that would be to argue against Romans 13, which clearly outlines how God has given the state the authority of the sword to punish those who do evil. Nevertheless, here's the key takeaway: God has given this authority to the state, not to the church. So let the state be the state. Let the state punish those who do evil (in humane, just, and restorative ways, of course). And let the church use its prophetic voice in the public square to peacefully advocate with the state (the God-ordained bearer of the sword) on behalf of victims of injustice and oppression in order that all roads be transformed to protect vulnerable travelers from being exploited in the first place.

Churches Fighting Cheap Justice

Whether we realize it or not, the Spirit of God is always on the move, renewing all things, including in the Western church. As I've worked to resource churches across the United States and Canada in prioritizing justice Jesus's way over the past decade, I've seen firsthand the Holy Spirit embolden church leaders to resist the allures of cheap justice while prioritizing justice Jesus's way. Here are just some of their stories.

Westside King's Church in Calgary, Alberta (Canada), has a goal of giving away 10 percent of their annual budget to justice work locally and globally. While a goal like this is truly commendable, Pastors Christine Woods and David Harvey don't want their church to fall into the trap of simply relegating their church community's justice work to contributing a percentage of their annual budgets; they want justice to be woven into the ethos of their community.

Again, I want to pause here to acknowledge how truly remarkable it is for a church to designate 10 percent of its annual budget toward justice work. It's quite rare for US or Canadian churches to set aside this much of their budgets for justice partnerships. But the pastors and leadership team of this church community also don't wish for this 10 percent earmark to hinder their own personal pursuit of justice Jesus's way. For these church leaders, justice is not just a line item but a whole way of being. To this end, instead of "one-way mission partnerships," Westside King's Church seeks "dialogical justice partnerships," these are partnerships based on a relationship of mutuality that allow their community to be shaped by their justice partners and those on the margins who they serve. They also make an intentional effort to include a focus on justice within the liturgy, teaching, and flow of their church services. For this congregation, every Sunday is invariably about justice. It is not a side pursuit.

Similarly, Southridge Community Church in Niagara, Ontario, devotes 72 percent of their total budget (which includes regional government grants for services for their unhoused neighbors) to local and global justice and compassion efforts. You read that right: 72 percent! This, of course, comes with major challenges. The Sunday morning service teams often feel like they're operating on a shoestring budget. But this justice-oriented church community makes an intentional choice to prioritize justice for their marginalized neighbors.

Nathan Dirks, the action pastor at Southridge who oversees much of its justice work, says, "Actually, not long ago, a church leadership team was visiting us and was pointing out all of the things about our facilities that would be unacceptable at their church. . . . They were really bothered by how lousy our parking lots are!"[4]

Pastor Deve Persad helps to lead Sarnia Evangelical Missionary Church in Sarnia, Ontario. Over the past two decades, he has faithfully shepherded this modest community of a couple hundred faithful Christians to care deeply about local and global justice issues—so much so that their church even launched a local organization to combat sex trafficking in their border town. So when Pastor Deve invited me to preach on the justice of Jesus at his church, I knew I had to make the three-hour drive from my home in the greater Toronto area to visit this unique community.

The first thing I noticed when I walked into the church's spacious sanctuary was the old, ugly bright orange carpet. I noticed this because ugly bright orange stands out. And this wasn't just an ugly bright orange carpet; it was an *ancient* ugly bright orange carpet, easily from the past century. "I know it's ugly, but our community tolerates it so that we can prioritize justice with our limited resources," I remember Pastor Deve telling me. That's right: The members know exactly how much it would cost to replace this ugly orange shag rug. But they also know exactly how much prioritizing justice Jesus's way costs, which is basically everything. So instead of focusing on church growth, they focus on faithfulness. And instead of focusing on the ugly orange shag rug, they focus on the ugly reality of injustice in their community and around the world.

"We're a bit quirky for some Christians in our town. But that's okay; we'd rather be faithful," Pastor Deve went on to tell me.

I've known Pastor Deve long enough to know that he also walks the walk. This is why he went three-fourths time at his church a few years ago to help his small congregation free up its budget to further prioritize justice.

Canadian churches like Southridge Community Church, Westside King's, and Sarnia Evangelical Missionary Church are serious about justice Jesus's way: the kind of justice that costs us something.

In May 2020, after George Floyd was killed, Rev. Matthew Murphy of Milltown, New Jersey, embarked on a journey of listening, learning, and shepherding his community to respond to their Black neighbors' cries for racial justice. When he was invited to say a few words and pray at a local Black Lives Matter rally in town along with other clergy, Pastor Matthew faithfully chose to show up. He says, "I put on my clerical collar and went. Many of our community leaders were in attendance, but what stood out to me was that none of our police, nor any of my white friends, were there. I posted about my attendance on social media and the need to deal with racism."[5]

Needless to say, the pushback Pastor Matthew (a white male evangelical pastor) experienced was visceral. Parishioners claimed he "hated" white people. People left the church. Rumors about his wife and children were spread across the congregation. Still, he went out of his way to meet with the dissenting community members. This only made things worse, as he found that those who were most vocal in their criticisms simply used this attempt at opening the lines of communication to further bolster their claims against him.

This story is by no account the first of its kind I've come across. Nor will it be the last. When church leaders like Pastor Matthew join the redemptive justice work of Jesus by resisting the powers and principalities of darkness, they are upsetting the old order of things to usher in God's new creation. And as I'd often hear people saying back when I worked in Georgia Republican politics, "Hit dogs holler."

Churches and ministries that seriously engage in the work of justice must be ready to pay the price of infuriating the powers and principalities and those within the church that benefit from them, even if that includes losing members and money in the short run. North American church and ministry leaders who pursue the justice of Jesus stand on the shoulders of many across the historical global church who have gone before us in this prophetic work of speaking truth to power on behalf of our marginalized neighbors.

Óscar Romero's Fight Against Cheap Justice

Church leaders like Pastor Matthew remind me of St. Óscar Romero, archbishop of San Salvador, the beautiful capital of El Salvador.

While Archbishop Romero is considered by many to be the patron saint of liberation theology today, like many Western church leaders in the present day (and like myself, when I worked in the American political world), Romero wasn't always on the side of marginalized and oppressed communities. In fact, up until the assassination of his friend and fellow priest, Rutilio Grande Garcia, Romero was mostly hesitant to get the church involved in "political matters"—specifically the human rights abuses and violence of the El Salvadoran government of the 1970s.

But once injustice hit closer to home with the murder of his friend, Romero vocally spoke out against the violent human rights atrocities being committed by his government. His sermons proclaiming the gospel of Christ as good news for victims of violence in his country were broadcast to thousands via radio across El Salvador each week.

Soon, Romero started receiving strong opposition for proclaiming the just and liberating gospel of Jesus of Nazareth. In addition to receiving several anonymous death threats, Romero also had to deal with being ostracized by fellow priests and bishops in the Catholic Church. But despite being frequently (and inaccurately) labeled a communist, he persisted in fighting for truth, justice, and peace. He even publicly critiqued Western empires like the United States for sending weapons to his country's oppressive regime.

Romero was assassinated by armed gunmen while presiding over Mass at a hospital for terminally ill patients on March 24, 1980. In an interview just five days before he was killed, he forgave and blessed his killers in advance, adding, "A bishop will die, but the Church of God, which is the people, will never perish."[6]

Romero's words came to pass. Decades after his assassination, the church in El Salvador and around the world has continued to preserve his legacy by persevering in the work of justice.

Despite his upstanding life, Romero continues to be a controversial figure within the Catholic Church. Despite being martyred for his witness, he was only canonized as a saint in 2018, largely because of concerns that his canonization would be seen as an endorsement of communism (even though Romero never identified as a communist).[7]

Romero's life and legacy remind me of Jesus's words in the Beatitudes: "Blessed are you when people revile you and persecute you and utter all kinds of evil against you falsely on my account. Rejoice and be glad, for your reward is great in heaven, for in the same way they persecuted the prophets who were before you" (Matt. 5:11–12).

Christians who are seeking justice for our marginalized neighbors today must not be surprised when resistance inevitably comes our way. And we must be prepared to deny our preference for cheap justice, to take up our cross and pay the cost of just discipleship.

Just Discipleship Is Worth the Trouble

During my stint as a Republican political consultant years ago, in what feels like another lifetime, I worked as a media consultant for a client who was running for Congress. The year was 2017. At that time, the race he was running in was the most expensive congressional race in the history of the United States. In the midst of that highly competitive context, I was asked to ghostwrite an opinion article on his behalf, arguing against immigration.

To be clear, the article I was tasked with writing was to oppose immigration in all its forms, including legal immigration. And to be even more clear, I was asked to oppose a specific legal pathway for immigration to the United States called the Diversity Immigrant Visa Program (DIVP).

Now if you know anything about me, you're probably picking up on the layers of irony here. *I* was a legal immigrant to the United States—specifically one whose family was a beneficiary of the DIVP. So naturally, I did what any up-and-coming political consultant without a moral compass does: I betrayed my values and cashed in for the big bucks. But the next day I woke up thinking, *What have I done? Who have I become? I should be terrified of myself! I ghost-wrote an opinion article for a congressional candidate basically saying that I should not be allowed to move to America.* Lord have mercy.

I shared this episode and the ensuing existential crisis with a friend, a wise older Christian woman I was working with on another state-level campaign. I remember telling her, "I really don't know what to do. I got into politics because of my passion for Jesus and because of my passion for justice. But here I am, selling my soul to the highest bidder. What do I do?"

I'll never forget the way she looked me in the eye with a calm smile and said, "Joash, I think you know what you need to do. You know exactly what you need to do." I often call this moment my personal encounter with Jesus on my Emmaus road.

We find the biblical analog recorded in the Gospel of Luke. Here is how it begins: "Now on that same day two of them [i.e., the disciples] were going to a village called Emmaus, about seven miles from Jerusalem" (Luke 24:13). Note that these disciples were going from Jerusalem to Emmaus. In other words, they were headed *away* from Jerusalem and the other disciples. But even though they were going in the wrong direction, we see the resurrected Jesus joining them. Verse 15 says, "While they were talking and discussing, Jesus himself came near and went with them. But their eyes were kept from recognizing him."

This is like an episode of *Undercover Boss*. A boss sees two employees headed down a path he does not wish them to take and joins them while hiding his identity. Jesus proceeds to do what an undercover boss wading into a conversation between two confused employees does. He asks them what they're talking about, and in response the two disciples start to talk to Jesus about Jesus. But they say something very interesting in verse 21 (something I would not have caught if it weren't for my friend Sarah Bessey's excellent book, *Field Notes for the Wilderness*[8]): "We had hoped that he was the one to redeem Israel." You can almost sense the depths of their disappointment in that utterance. Their expectation was that Jesus would redeem Israel. But instead, he was crucified. Maybe you resonate with that.

"We had hoped that moving here would be different. But instead, life is tougher than ever before."

"I had hoped that this relationship or friendship would be different. But instead, it disappointed me like every other relationship."

"I had hoped that this job or this career or business opportunity would be different. But instead, pursuing it was the worst decision of my life."

"We had hoped that the doctor's diagnosis would be different. But instead, we just have more bad news."

"We had hoped that this church would be different. But instead, we ended up with more church trauma."

Or maybe, like these disciples, you had hoped for something from God and instead found yourself disappointed. And you found yourself walking in the wrong direction because of your disappointment in life and with God. Maybe you once had hopes and dreams and watched as those hopes and dreams crashed and burned. And if you're being totally honest with yourself, maybe you find yourself wondering if this whole Jesus thing is real and worth it.

Here's the good news: The God who commands us to seek justice, love mercy, and walk humbly with him comes down to earth to join us and show us *how* to walk humbly with him. By the end of their journey on the road to Emmaus, we see the disciples breaking bread with Jesus. And it's in breaking bread with Jesus that they recognize him as Jesus. And then he is gone.

But remember that Jesus walks with them *in the wrong direction* and breaks bread with them until they recognize him. And once they recognize him, here's how the disciples respond: "That same hour, they got up and returned to Jerusalem" (Luke 24:33).

Did you catch that? *That same hour* they get up and start walking humbly with God in the right direction. And they go and join God and God's people in creating a new community that will partner with the Spirit in pursuing the kingdom of God, on earth as it is in heaven.

Maybe you resonate with this story because, like the disciples, as soon as life got tough, you made choices to walk in the wrong direction. Maybe it's with personal decisions. Or maybe it's with business decisions or financial decisions in which you chose to build your own empire. Or where you decided to only take care of yourself and look out for your own interests instead of prioritizing justice for all of our marginalized neighbors.

If that's you, Jesus is inviting you to walk humbly with God by pursuing justice in a new way—a way that actually costs you. But know this: Jesus will keep walking with you even if you're moving in the wrong direction. He will remain beside you, encouraging you to start walking in the direction of doing justice, loving kindness, and walking humbly with him.

In a Western world that is obsessed with fighting for "my rights," "my comforts," and "my privileges," disciples of Jesus are called to be a counterculturral voice in the wilderness, crying out, "Take my rights, take my comforts, and take my privileges for the healing of this world." I don't think it's a coincidence that the disciples only recognize Jesus at the Eucharistic table. And I don't think it's a coincidence that the disciples turn around and go back to Jerusalem after Jesus breaks the bread and (presumably) says, "The body of Christ broken for you."

The body of Christ was broken to make us whole; and through our wholeness, we extend the offer of wholeness to others. We, the church, are meant to be the body of Christ broken for the healing and wholeness of this world. Are we living in a way that costs us something but is healing to the world?

I know that you care about justice, but maybe you don't know what it actually means to pursue and prioritize the justice of Jesus. So allow me to challenge you by asking: Is doing justice actually costing you something? Do you love your neighbor enough to give up your own comforts and luxuries? Or do you love your neighbor just enough that you'll do justice and love kindness as long it doesn't actually cost you anything?

Many years ago, Jesus met me on the road to Emmaus—or, in my case, on the road to Washington, DC. But he turned me around and put me on another path. This new path steered me away from power and toward helping people on the margins. And it also came with a 50 percent pay cut as I pivoted to a nonprofit job in human rights advocacy. I wonder if we all need to have an encounter (and perhaps more than one) with Jesus on the Emmaus road so we keep finding the courage to resist cheap justice and walk in the right direction: the direction of doing justice, loving mercy, and walking humbly with God.

The Western Church on the Road to Emmaus

So far, we have defined the justice of Jesus as prioritizing the welfare of others in the same way that the Good Samaritan did. We have also established that much of the Western church resists justice Jesus's way—the kind of justice that costs us. And we have examined the ways in which colonizer and slaveholder theological frameworks have shaped us to resist justice.

We have also established the tendencies of the Western church to prefer cheap justice, which is a kind of justice where we do the bare minimum and pat ourselves heartily on the back for it. It is clear that the way of the Western church is profoundly broken. And just as many of us individually need an encounter with Jesus on the road to Emmaus, I would argue that the Western church also collectively needs such an encounter with Jesus.

There is no doubt in my mind that so many who claim to be followers of Christ are walking in the wrong direction, away from the just and liberating gospel of Christ toward the unjust and subjugating gospel of colonizers and enslavers. Yes, Jesus still walks with us when we go in the wrong direction, but this isn't because of our faithfulness but rather because of God's love and kindness.

Close your eyes for a moment and envision Jesus as he says to the Western church: "Listen! I am standing at the door, knocking; if you hear my voice and open the door, I will come in and eat with you, and you with me" (Rev. 3:20). Will we as the church respond by opening the door and feasting with him? Or will we dig deep into our stubborn and hyper-individualistic ways to resist this invitation?

Turning from our unjust ways is only half the invitation. As someone who aspires to offer both critique and encouragement for the Western church, I can tell you from firsthand experience that while offering critique has its place, it is always the easy part. The real work lies in acknowledging and embodying a vision for walking with God (and with people and their messy lives) in the right direction after we encounter Jesus on the road to Emmaus.

Walter Brueggemann wisely writes, "The task of prophetic ministry is to nurture, nourish, and evoke a consciousness and perception alternative to the consciousness and perception of the dominant culture around us."[9] And this is exactly where I hope to try and take us in these next chapters, for the sake of the just and liberating gospel of Christ, which is indeed good news for the whole world, including our marginalized neighbors.

REFLECTION QUESTIONS

1. What has prioritizing the justice of Jesus cost you? How is justice Jesus's way costing you today? Or do you not really feel a cost?

2. If you are a church leader, is your pursuit of justice actually costing your church anything? If you are a church member, do you see your church prioritizing justice in ways that have a cost?
3. Do you love your marginalized neighbors enough to give up your comforts and luxuries? Or do you love your marginalized neighbors just enough that you'll seek justice for them as long it doesn't actually cost you anything?
4. What are some ways in which you (or your church) have been complicit in cheap justice? How is Jesus calling you to resist cheap justice and prioritize the justice of Jesus?

3

How Churches Today Are Prioritizing Justice

> I prefer a church which is bruised, hurting and dirty because it has been out on the streets, rather than a church which is unhealthy from being confined and from clinging to its own security.
>
> —Pope Francis, *The Joy of the Gospel*

What It Takes to Walk the Walk

"Our neighbors don't really care about how many missionaries our churches send. They care way more about our contribution to the common good."

These words from my friend Jeremy Johnson have stuck with me. Pastor Jeremy leads ministries and staff at Village Church, one of the largest, fastest-growing multisite churches in Canada. It's one of the flagship churches of its denomination, the Fellowship of Evangelical Baptists in Canada.

Pastor Jeremy and Village Church don't just talk the talk. Over the past decade, Village Church congregations have generously partnered with organizations to significantly reduce child sex trafficking across the world. They have raised millions of dollars for their partners via golf tournaments, budgeting, and Sunday service collections. And they have done this by regularly visiting their partners and several survivor leaders in the Global South—not by way of mission trips but via "vision trips," spending their time listening to local leaders and learning how their church can partner with them. (We will discuss the difference between mission trips and vision trips in chap. 9.)

I've visited Village Church and spoken to their community twice now. During my first visit, more than three hundred households signed up as monthly donors with one of their justice partners. During my second visit, eighteen months later, I spoke alongside a survivor of human trafficking. This was the first time Village Church had a survivor leader speak at their services. We saw a hundred more households sign up as monthly donors with this justice partner that Sunday.

Now many of you might read this, look up Village Church, and say, "But Joash, that's easy for a large church to do." This is fair pushback. But consider this: I've been mobilizing churches in the West to prioritize justice for a decade now. Believe me when I tell you that this level of generosity is unprecedented among large churches anywhere in the world. And believe me when I tell you that this level of generosity from a church community always comes with a cost: both at an individual and an organizational level.

In my experience, many large churches in the United States and Canada struggle with encouraging their people to give directly to justice and compassion organizations out of fears that they won't be able to meet their own needs. But the people of Village Church care deeply about their contribution to the common good. This generous community recognizes that to faithfully follow Jesus means making justice a priority—a priority that comes with a cost. But also, in the experience of their leadership, this is a priority that energizes their community and often unexpectedly begets more generosity toward their own needs.

Trinity Church Kelowna is no different. A North American Baptist church with about twenty-five hundred members, nestled in the lovely Canadian wine country of interior British Columbia, Trinity Church has partnered with organizations taking on labor trafficking and violence against women and children for almost two decades. Back in 2020, its main sanctuary was unexpectedly confronted with a flooding problem, resulting in damages costing more than half a million dollars. In 2023, coming out of the pandemic, Trinity Church decided to reengage with its justice and compassion partners. As part of this initiative, I was invited to visit and teach their congregation. Despite their own budgetary needs, Trinity generously agreed to fund a pilot legal-training program in trauma-informed care for over three hundred lawyers across Bolivia in partnership with the Bolivian Ministry of Justice and the United Nations Office on Drugs and Crime. I knew how costly this level of generosity was to the people and the leadership.

I was back preaching at Trinity a year later. The night before I preached, Pastor Scott Lanigan pulled me aside and, with tears in his eyes, said, "Committing to raise thousands of dollars for our justice and compassion partners this weekend is definitely an expensive, faith-fueled decision for our leadership team. We're still in the red financially because of our building repair debt. But there is no doubt in our hearts that to prioritize justice is why we exist as a church. Still, we have decided to just lean into prioritizing justice this weekend and to trust God to do his part to take care of our needs—just as he always has."

Village Church and Trinity Church are just two examples of Canadian churches that prioritize justice at great cost to themselves. What makes these churches unique is not just their sacrificial generosity but also how this generosity has come after they have taken a humble, listening posture in the course of building relationships with and learning from local leaders in the Global South.

Many years ago, I had the chance to sit with the Anglican bishop of one of the largest cities in South Asia. The Anglican Church in South Asia has a unique history; for centuries it helped perpetuate colonization, yet today it leads the charge on several justice issues, especially in the fight against child sex trafficking. They do this by running a number of rehabilitation homes for survivors of trafficking and by mobilizing dozens of volunteers to partner with organizations battling sex trafficking in their city, state, and country.

In 2023, I met with the Catholic Bishops' Conference of the Philippines in Manila. Again, much like my experience in South Asia, I heard story after story of how a major branch of the Western church that once oppressed Global South peoples was now reversing the tide of centuries of complicity by leading the charge against human trafficking and the online sexual exploitation of children across the Philippines.

The Catholic and Anglican churches' active efforts to repent of their past and prioritize justice across the Global South is inspiring. It's a big deal for any branch of the church to repent of its past shortcomings, but this is especially true in community-oriented, honor-shame cultures that make up much of the Global South.

Their commitment seems to me to be in direct obedience to the prophet Isaiah's words to a rebellious, unjust people of God: "Learn to do good; seek justice; rescue the oppressed; defend the orphan; plead for the widow" (Isa. 1:17).

What is the best way to resist the unjust and subjugating gospel of the colonizers? *Learn to do good.* What is the best way to resist the allures of cheap justice? *Seek justice for anyone in need of justice.* Begin with people who are oppressed, orphaned, and widowed.

In the case of the Catholic and Anglican churches, the cost of justice Jesus's way is being honest about and repentant of their history of participating in colonization, as well as correcting injustices often birthed out of colonization. Such injustices are frequently seen in decimated public infrastructure, such as sanitation, justice systems, and health care. Many aspects of public infrastructure were set up by colonial powers that had linked arms with the Western church and operated against the interests of the most vulnerable—especially women and children from marginalized and Indigenous communities.

Witnessing the courage of our Catholic and Anglican siblings in Christ in the Global South has me wondering: What if we saw the ecclesial and theological descendants of slaveholder and segregationist theologians in the United States (such as the Southern Baptist Convention, southern Anglicans, and southern Presbyterians) repent for the ways they have benefited from these historical and systemic injustices?

What would it look like for all of us in the majority-culture Western church, who have benefited from the sins of colonization, slavery, and segregation, to repent and address the aftereffects of these sins?

I say *us* because I too have benefited from colonization. Even though I was born and raised in the Global South, I became a beneficiary of colonization the day I moved to the West and started enjoying its advantages. The call to decolonize, repent, and prioritize justice is not a call to the white, majority-culture Western church alone. The call to decolonize is just as much a call to the immigrant, diaspora church across the West to examine the ways in which it now benefits from the colonial past of the nation where it now thrives. In this way, we can be faithful stewards of what we find ourselves entrusted with.

This calling is also why, as a fundraiser for justice organizations actively reversing the decimating effects of centuries of colonization in the Global South, I will never play down the need for Western resources for the work of justice.

Church leaders of various ethnicities often ask me, "Joash, what can our church communities do for justice work globally, apart from just giving?" I always appreciate this well-intentioned question. These leaders are absolutely correct to be concerned about their people reducing the work of justice to merely throwing a few dollars at the cause every year and patting themselves on the back.

But for us as Western Christians, it is of utmost importance to prioritize justice by giving away our wealth, especially given the history of how wealth was built in the West. Giving away our wealth in support of Global South communities whose ancestors were robbed by colonization is not the only thing we can do to prioritize the justice of Jesus, but it must be the first thing we do.

The Church of England and the Transatlantic Slave Trade

In January 2023, leaders of the Church of England announced that they had learned their eighteenth-century forebears had invested in and profited from a shipping company that transported thousands of people into slavery.[1] The investigation was initiated by Church Commissioners, a charity managing the church's investment portfolio. It looked into the church's investment fund, once known as Queen Anne's Bounty. They learned that by 1777, Queen Anne's Bounty had investments worth £406,942 (the equivalent of around £724 million or $920 million today) in the South Sea Company.[2] That's a lot of church money invested in the transatlantic slave trade.

The commissioners also discovered that the church had deliberately ignored the cries of several people in slavery who wrote to them. But the cries of people in slavery and oppression always reach God. And every injustice against our marginalized neighbors will eventually come to light.

In response to this news, the Church of England announced the intention to create a £100 million fund to address past wrongs. The Associated Press reports Church Commissioners chief executive Gareth Mostyn as saying, "This isn't about paying compensation to individuals, and it's not really just about the money. . . . No amount of money will ever be enough to repair the damage done through the trans-Atlantic slave trade. . . . But we hope that our response will be a means of investing in a better future for all." Mostyn went on to call these funds an investment in the Church of England's "journey of repentance."[3]

Even though the Church of England steered clear of "reparations" language, these designated funds are reparative in nature and will prioritize community projects addressing the aftermath of slavery. After all, if justice is indeed giving to each person their due, as defined by Augustine, the allocation of these funds to support communities robbed of their futures through the transatlantic slave trade is just one way to pursue justice for these communities.

The then-archbishop of Canterbury, Justin Welby, said it was "time to take action to address our shameful past."[4] Not surprisingly, the Anglican Church's commitment received significant pushback. One critic, the chair of a prominent advocacy group within the Church of England, wrote an open letter to Archbishop Welby, countering, "Before the Church can find £100 million for this new project, it needs to show that it can sort its own house out and fund its frontline."[5]

Notice how this leader doesn't consider community reparations for the church's past participation in the sin of slavery an act of "sorting its own house out." And note how he doesn't consider correcting the past sin of injustice as "frontline" work (which he classifies as preserving dying parishes in the Church of England). We see once again the prioritization of the salvation of souls at the cost of the liberation of human bodies—the spiritual over the physical.

This raises a question: Where does this anemic understanding of "the front line" come from? And could this broken understanding of the front line exist because so many Western church leaders have not examined the theological frameworks they've inherited from the slaveholder-enabling, modern-era Church of England, Dutch Reformed Church, Roman Catholic Church, and Southern Baptist Convention?

If the just and liberating gospel of Christ is indeed good news for people in poverty and oppression, as Jesus declares in Luke 4:18, our definition of the frontline work of the church will not simply *include* justice for our marginalized neighbors; it will *center on* justice for our marginalized neighbors.

It's only fair to expect today's Western church to step up and partner with the Global South church in alleviating the aftereffects of colonialism. This is especially true because majority world churches are more limited in their ability to address these needs, given the economic inequalities between the West and the Global South (another aftereffect of Western colonization and imperialism).

Indigenous leaders in the Global South know exactly what their countries need. They have the leadership and expertise to fight the injustices plaguing their countries and communities. They just need resources to help address them: resources that, for historical reasons, happen to be concentrated in the West.

I cannot help wondering what Zacchaeus would say to the Western church today. So many of us have been raised to think of him simply in terms of his stature as a "wee little man." But Zacchaeus was more than a "short king." He was a widely despised tax collector, an oppressor, and an agent of the Roman Empire.

But what does Zacchaeus do when Jesus shows him radical grace and inclusion? He tells Jesus, "Look, half of my possessions, Lord, I will give to the poor, and if I have defrauded anyone of anything, I will pay back four times as much" (Luke 19:8).

Maybe you're reading this as someone who is skeptical of the Church of England's decision to give away its stolen wealth. Maybe in the same way that cynical religious leaders of Jesus's time rejected his teaching, the polarized environment of the West has conditioned many of us and our neighbors to callously respond to redemptive stories like this with "that's just 'woke' Marxism creeping into the church." If that's you, I want to invite you to wrestle with Zacchaeus's encounter with Jesus in Luke 19. Assigning a modern political label to biblically precedented acts of justice has become a kneejerk reaction that both institutions and individuals use to let themselves off the hook.

It's time we, the Western church, get serious about reparative, restorative justice because reparative, restorative justice is the way of Jesus. And as we see in the story of Zacchaeus in the Gospel of Luke, reparative, restorative justice is profoundly biblical.

The Diaspora Immigrant Church in the West

When it comes to justice, one overlooked segment of the church in the West is the diaspora immigrant church. So much of the West today consists of immigrant communities that have moved from Global South countries to the West in pursuit of better economic and educational opportunities. As someone who is part of one of the largest diaspora immigrant communities, I have physically felt the spike of anti-immigrant hatred against communities like mine in North America over the past few years. Given the historical context at play here, I believe it is only fair that formerly colonized communities be welcomed to partake in the benefits of the wealth that was stolen from their ancestors to enrich Western economies.

With these diaspora immigrant communities, spread throughout the West, also come diaspora immigrant church leaders who care for their spiritual and physical needs. As someone who has closely participated in Indian, Filipino, and Caribbean churches in the United States and Canada, I have been greatly encouraged by the bend toward justice these communities advocate for in the West.

Gone are the days when global missions was about churches in the West exporting their practice of Western Christianity to the Global South. Global missions in 2025 look entirely different from missionary work even twenty years ago. In my opinion, the new wave of global missions comes from the Holy Spirit strengthening a Western church in decline by infusing a passion for the proclamation of the whole, just, and liberating gospel of Christ through the diaspora immigrant church.

Global South Christians, like my family members, end up immigrating to the West in search of economic and educational opportunities—again, because of the ways in which the West has benefited from centuries of colonization. But we don't come to the West with a hard heart toward justice. If anything, Global South Christians who have experienced physical oppression in more tangible ways than their white, Western siblings are well aware that the gospel of Christ is just, liberating, and inclusive. And we are well aware that the gospel of Christ will never be received by our Global South neighbors if it is purely perceived as spiritual in nature.

Pastor Paul Berenguer is the lead pastor of Champion Life Centre in Brampton, a Toronto suburb often colloquially referred to as Brown Town because of its predominantly South Asian Punjabi population. Originally launched as a majority-Filipino Pentecostal church by Pastor Paul's father, Champion Life Centre has strengthened dozens of local churches in Canada and across the world. For Champion Life leaders, providing their communities with opportunities to prioritize justice and compassion is a top priority, and giving financially is an important part of this. Champion Life leaders find the work of justice to be critical to their credibility and witness as twenty-first-century Christians. This is especially true in their engagement with second-generation immigrant Christians in their churches and their friends at university and work.

Pastor Paul once said to me, "Because Champion Life Centre is predominantly composed of immigrants, the participation and support of justice work both locally and globally is an important part of our ministry. Many of us share common ground with people who have faced oppression and have been impacted by injustice. We can't help but look to extend what we have experienced (in Christ) to others."

The Spirit may also be strengthening the Western church through immigrant communities owing to the rise of Pentecostalism in the Global South. In fact, the only growing evangelical denomination in both the United States and Canada at the time of this book's writing is the Assemblies of God and Pentecostal Assemblies of Canada. And immigration is the major contributing factor, as many Global South evangelicals immigrating to the West look to join Pentecostal immigrant or (majority-white) multiethnic churches—just as my parents did when we moved from India to the United States in 2011.

Global South Christians (especially Pentecostals, like those at Champion Life Centre) don't need to be convinced of the role of justice in Christian mission. We simply cannot effectively proclaim the gospel of Christ in our Global South contexts without first talking about its just and liberating nature. And we don't need to be persuaded of the reality of injustice. We've seen its prevalence firsthand due to the effects of centuries of Western colonization in our home countries. And Pentecostal Global South Christians in particular see the Holy

Spirit mobilizing and equipping churches to address the physical needs of their marginalized neighbors. This is why Pentecostals place a heavy emphasis on praying for physical healing and financial well-being. But diaspora immigrant Christians in the West are not just Pentecostal and evangelical. They are also Catholic, Orthodox, Anglican, and Mar Thoma (a major branch of St. Thomas Indian Christianity that is also in the Anglican Communion).

I've sat with Filipino leaders in Canada and Italy who have told me how Filipino Catholics are now the largest demographic of parishioners and tithers in many parts of the West, a situation similar to that of Latin Americans in the US Catholic Church.

I've sat with Coptic Egyptian Orthodox and Indian Orthodox priests and bishops in North America who have shared how their communities are actively growing to the point where they're running out of space because of an influx of Christian immigrants.

I've sat with Mar Thoma church leaders in Toronto who have told me about not having enough clergy to support all the church planting and growth work taking place due to Mar Thoma Christians immigrating here from India and the Middle East.

And I've sat with Anglican leaders in Toronto who have told me about their church communities becoming stronger and more diverse with the increased immigration of Anglicans from Africa and India.

I've engaged all of these leaders in conversations about justice because these Global South Christians are highly justice oriented. The story of diaspora immigrant Christians strengthening the Western church is one that is still being written. But I wouldn't be surprised if the Western church became more justice oriented, diverse, and inclusive because of the influx of Global South Christians.

The Black American Church

After I experienced racial trauma in the white American church in 2020, what saved my faith was not attending one of the world's leading evangelical seminaries. What saved my faith was attending Black churches in the US South, listening to Black preachers online, and watching the sustained courage and perseverance of the Black American church in the aftermath of the unjust killings of George Floyd, Ahmaud Arbery, and Breonna Taylor.

The Black American church has a legacy of being both faithful to Jesus and vocal about justice despite centuries of systemic oppression and marginalization, ranging from the transatlantic slave trade to lynchings and Jim Crow segregation all the way to modern forms of systemic racism and anti-Blackness.

By producing witnesses and advocates like Martin Luther King Jr., Harriet Tubman, James Cone, Shirley Chisholm, and many more, the Black church shows us what it looks like to embody Jesus and his just, liberating ways in a broken, unjust world. I tell all my progressive, deconstructing white friends in the Western church not to give up on Jesus until they have first exposed themselves to alternative, faithful, and justice-seeking Christian traditions such as the Black church. The Black church provides Western Christianity with a model of resisting the allures of "empire" (the unjust political fiefdoms of man that stand in stark contrast to the just kingdom of God made known to us through Jesus) while being faithful to Jesus. I believe that Black Christians can revitalize the Western church and show us the way forward—if we humble ourselves and learn from them.

Keep in mind that the American Empire was never really built with Black Americans in mind as equal citizens. This is because empires are never set up with their marginalized neighbors' flourishing in mind. By their very nature, empire economies operate with the explicit intention of concentrating power and privilege in the hands of a few, often to the detriment of those who occupy the lower rungs of the social hierarchy. Despite the Declaration of Independence claiming that all men are created equal and endowed by their Creator with certain unalienable rights, in practice Black Americans were materially refused these rights for centuries. The Black church joyfully and soulfully resisted this empire mindset by holding to what it knew to be divinely true: They were equal in the eyes of God, even if their white neighbors refused to acknowledge this reality.

The Black American church is also evidence of God redeeming for good what the enemy has meant for evil. Or in Jemar Tisby's words, "Harsh though it may sound, the facts of history nevertheless bear out this truth: there would be no black church without racism in the white church."[6]

The Black American church taught me to humble myself, to put aside my male, Asian American privilege, and to sit at the feet of those more marginalized to experience Jesus and his solidarity with people in oppression today. As an advocate for justice, I find myself rereading James Cone and Black liberation theology any time I wrestle with God's goodness in the face of injustice and oppression. Black liberation theology is, after all, theology from the margins of society—theology that recognizes the beauty of God and his just and liberating gospel while also acknowledging and lamenting the reality of Black suffering and oppression.

Because of the work I do, which is the work of mobilizing the Western church to come alongside Global South Christians in the work of justice, I am certainly privileged to know personally all these positive examples of churches prioritizing justice today.

It is completely understandable to feel jaded about the Christian faith because of the witness of large swaths of the Western church that have inherited their theology from church leaders who were okay with subjugating their Global South neighbors through slavery and colonization. But to envision a way forward, we must learn from Christians on the margins who have faithfully resisted the allures of empire. This includes the Black American church and the diaspora immigrant church, along with other groups on the margins of the Western church, such as the Anabaptist tradition.

We Western Christians have a unique opportunity to humble ourselves and sit at the feet of our siblings in Christ around the world (including right here in the West) who prioritize justice in meaningful and effective ways.

REFLECTION QUESTIONS

1. What lessons can we learn from churches that are actively repenting of their unjust ways and prioritizing justice today—like the Anglican Church in South Asia, the Catholic Church in the Philippines, and the Church of England?
2. What lessons can we learn from the faithful witness of the diaspora immigrant church and the Black American church?
3. How can we humble ourselves, cultivate curiosity, and sit at the feet of these siblings in Christ to learn from them—especially when the colonizer's gospel has taught us to ignore and decenter them?
4. How does this chapter inspire you to prioritize the justice of Jesus (both individually and communally)?

PART 2

DECOLONIZING THE WESTERN CHURCH

4

Decolonizing Our Theology

> When a society's Christian faith—born from colonized and serially enslaved Brown people—does not cause that society to challenge and reject slavery outright, then there is a problem with the construction of that faith. To save our faith we must decolonize it.
>
> —Lisa Sharon Harper, foreword to
> *If God Still Breathes, Why Can't I?*

The Christian faith, as much as it is a historical faith, was never meant to be a stagnant faith. It is meant to be embodied and uniquely applied to the contexts we find ourselves in today. Palestinian Catholic theologian Rafiq Khoury portrays this tension as a battle of two "memories": a closed memory and a creative memory, or what he calls "memory as a prison" and "memory as prophecy." Memory as a prison is one that "could mummify us in a certain time and place and prevent us from getting out of it." Memory as a prison inhibits us from creatively imagining a new reality. On the other hand, memory as prophecy is "a stimulant" that helps us "go forward and invent a new future and a new untold narrative."[1]

Palestinian pastor Mitri Raheb connects these ideas to the work of biblical interpretation. He writes, "The one who interprets [the Bible] assumes power; the one who dominates the story makes it his-story, her-story, literally creating history."[2] This is why, in order for us to reimagine a just and liberating future for the Western church, we must first decolonize our theologies of the narratives and ways of empire. And decolonizing our pulpits is a big part of decolonizing our theology.

Decolonizing Our Pulpits

One of the core tenets of the colonizer's gospel, which we unpacked in chapter 1, is that *social hierarchies are natural and part of God's design*. The colonizer's gospel prefers to structure the church (and human society) around authority and hierarchy. The institutional church can be a key weapon in the hands of an empire to reiterate its vision of authority and control. And the best way for an empire to reinforce its propaganda is through the power of the pulpit.

We know this to be true from the history of the Western church—whether it's the Roman Catholic Church becoming a tool for the Roman Empire; various European churches becoming tools for the medieval Christendom empires; the Dutch Reformed, Anglican, and Roman Catholic churches becoming tools for Western colonizing empires; the German church becoming a tool for the Nazi Third Reich; or the US Southern church becoming a tool for the Confederate Empire. Each of these are examples of historical empires that weaponized church pulpits in the active oppression of their neighbors.

The weaponization of the pulpit for the advancement of an empire and its propaganda still persists in the Western church today. Perhaps this is why many of us in the Western church who care deeply about justice find ourselves disillusioned by many North American evangelical Christians' apathy to the loss of thousands of children's lives in Gaza. In an ideal world, the Western church's quickness to condemn the October 7 terrorist attacks of Hamas on Israel should have been followed by its immediate condemnation of the Israeli government's indiscriminate mass murder of thousands of civilians in Gaza—especially women and children. But much of the North American church's slowness to speak out on the latter should alert us that something deeper is at play in both the institutional conservative and progressive Western church—something our Palestinian siblings in Christ have been alerting us to for decades now. Western empires (like the American Empire) play a key role in influencing Western church pulpits on wars, which prioritize geopolitical interests over saving lives.

As a preacher, I can attest firsthand that pulpits have power. Whether we like it or not, people in pulpits have tremendous influence over how biblical texts are interpreted. And if we're only accustomed to hearing from people with power and privilege in the pulpit (a demographic that also happens to be empire's favorite group of preachers), we will miss out on hearing from faithful voices on the margins. And we will miss out on hearing from God.

Jesus once said, "Give to Caesar the things that are Caesar's and to God the things that are God's" (Mark 12:17). Many of us in the Western church would be content with only applying this text to taxes and tithes. You have probably even heard this text interpreted in this way by pastors and preachers in Western pulpits. Nevertheless, I think Jesus was getting at something much deeper than just this. Because if we truly believe that the earth is the Lord's and that everything in it belongs to the Lord, as Psalm 24:1 teaches, we will interpret these words of Jesus as meaning, "We belong to the Lord and thus must give all of ourselves to God."

The caesars and empires of today (especially partisan politicians in the West) would cleverly have us prefer only certain sets of marginalized neighbors (like the unborn, working-class white Westerners, Jewish people, etc.), while advocating against other marginalized neighbors (immigrant families, Palestinian people, refugees etc.) who are sometimes considered "enemies of the empire." But justice Jesus's way stands in stark contrast to justice empire's way because the former includes the marginalized groups that empire prioritizes as well as the marginalized groups that empire wants the church to hate. In my ordination vows as a deacon in the Anglican/Episcopalian tradition, I vowed to bring to the church the needs and hopes of *all* the people. Because the justice of Jesus and the gospel of Jesus is good news to *all* of humankind, the church must also resist the narrow ways of empire by prioritizing justice for *all* our marginalized neighbors.

Following are a few ways for the Western church to prioritize justice (regardless of who it's for) by decolonizing our pulpits.

Centering Marginalized Teachers in the Pulpit

OneChurch.to is one of the largest, fastest-growing Pentecostal churches in Canada. Based in the greater Toronto area, it is easily the most multiethnic church I have ever preached at. Like Champion Life Centre (discussed in chap. 3), the predominantly immigrant community at OneChurch.to cares deeply about justice for their marginalized neighbors—both in Toronto and around the world.

I will never forget my first conversation with lead pastor Jonathan David Smith. Over sumptuous masala dosas (life-changing spicy south-Indian rice pancakes), Pastor Jonathan told me about his deep love for his authentically multiethnic, multicultural church community. He also identified a key challenge his leadership team was facing: the task of inspiring gifted, non-white immigrant voices from the community to be trained and positioned as leaders and teachers on their ministry team. Pastor Jonathan and his team wanted me to guest preach at their church as often as possible until they could meet this need internally.

Pastor Jonathan went on to share exciting details about a multiyear plan that would help his community raise more immigrant teachers, preachers, and ministry leaders. One of their first steps would be to partner with their denomination's seminary to make seminary training more accessible to the immigrant communities represented at OneChurch.to.

The reality so many of us forget is that marginalized people and the Western church experience Jesus and his good news in very different ways. Howard Thurman was a Black American theologian and civil rights leader who had perhaps the greatest influence on Martin Luther King Jr.'s theology. Thurman makes the point this way:

> The basic fact is that Christianity as it was born in the mind of this Jewish teacher and thinker [Jesus] appears as a technique of survival for the oppressed. That it became, through the intervening years, a religion of the powerful and the dominant, used sometimes as an instrument of oppression, must not tempt us into believing that it was thus in the mind and life of Jesus. "In him was life; and the life was the light of men." Wherever his spirit appears, the oppressed gather fresh courage; for he announced the good news that fear, hypocrisy, and hatred, the three hounds of hell that track the trail of the disinherited, need have no dominion over them.[3]

I cannot think of a more effective way to dispose of a bootleg version of Christianity that proclaims primarily "good news for the powerful" than by recentering the voices of our oppressed neighbors in the pulpit. Doing this will also help us recover the original "good news for the oppressed" version of Christianity, which Jesus and the early church taught and embodied.

Imagine someone significantly different from you teaching you about Jesus from a text you have read a thousand times before. Because they are so different from you and because their experience of suffering has been so different from yours, their experience of Jesus amid suffering is something you have likely never heard preached before. And the gospel—the just and liberating gospel of Jesus of Nazareth—seems fresh and sweet to you all over again, just like the first time you heard it.

All metaphors ultimately fall short when we're talking about this just and liberating gospel of Christ, but let me try one nonetheless. I've heard Ed Sheeran's music a thousand times on the radio and on Spotify. It's good, but it's never quite been *my thing*. Yet I recently saw a clip on social media of Sheeran performing with Punjabi pop singer Diljit Dosanjh where the two were blending some of their music. I will never be able to listen to Sheeran's music the same way again, all because of that clip of that one artistic collaboration. This is also what happens with the just and liberating gospel of Jesus when sung to us by marginalized people who have experienced Jesus in the midst of their physical oppression. It just "hits different."

I've been around the institutional church long enough to have heard many gifted preachers from across the world; some of them have even pastored me at one time or another. I've heard seminary lectures taught by some of the most knowledgeable Bible teachers in the world. But all of these teachers and experiences pale in comparison to a singular occasion when I asked a survivor of child sex trafficking in the Philippines about why she chose to follow Jesus despite the deep trauma she endured. Her personal story was one of the most powerful, uplifting, and unforgettable messages I have ever heard. If you've never heard the liberation of Jesus proclaimed by someone who has experienced it firsthand, you're missing out.

To be clear, I'm not saying that we need to replace all our majority-culture pastors and church leaders with pastors and leaders from marginalized communities. We need a broad range of voices, and inclusion by exclusion is not the way of Jesus. Besides, this would also be highly unrealistic, as there simply aren't enough people from marginalized communities who are called and trained as leaders to fill every pulpit across the Western church. Marginalized voices are on the margins for a reason, and it will take time and intentionality to equip them so that they can confidently speak as leaders in their own right.

Majority-culture pastors and church leaders can, however, make a concerted effort to ensure that their communities are directly exposed to the experiences and perspectives of their marginalized neighbors. This can be done from the pulpit in a variety of ways: ranging from live or recorded interviews to guest preachers to quoting marginalized voices from the pulpit on a regular basis. This endeavor is necessary because a church that is not shaped by the margins cannot faithfully proclaim good news to people in poverty, captivity, and oppression.

Recentering the Table

My friend Johnna Harris made the following comment during the course of a recent conversation: "I feel like progressive ex-vangelicals form their own church communities only to rinse and repeat strategies and tactics they learned from their previous conservative fundamentalist churches." Johnna hosts the podcast *Bodies Behind the Bus*, which features spiritual abuse survivors. The podcast is named after the now-infamous words of Pastor Mark Driscoll: "There is a pile of dead bodies behind the Mars Hill bus, and by God's grace, it'll be a mountain by the time we're done. You either get on the bus or you get run over by the bus. Those are the two options, but the bus ain't gonna stop."[4]

When we prioritize the salvation of souls over the liberation of human bodies, we (church and ministry leaders) say bizarre things that sound nothing like the way of Jesus. During my recent conversations with Johnna, she and I found we are of the same mind; until and unless we stop to take a hard look under the hood of "the bus" (the institutional church), we will continue seeing more people being thrown under it. And the best way to avoid piling up bodies behind the bus is to stop and fix the darn bus. Unfortunately, many progressive exvangelicals rush to plant attractional churches that look, feel, and sound like the rudderless evangelical churches they just left. The theology may be different, but the structures of power and uniformity are more or less the same.

Deconstruction without decolonization is pointless and ultimately does nothing for our marginalized neighbors. And to decolonize the Western church, we must start by decentering the pulpit and recentering the Table (known as the Eucharistic Table or the Communion Table in many Christian traditions). In other words, we must take the focus off the preacher and center it on Jesus.

There are two places I've truly experienced Jesus—the Table and the margins. As a global advocacy leader regularly interacting with people on the margins, I have clearly experienced Jesus on the margins. But I've also experienced Jesus at the Table when I've participated in the Eucharist. Up until the Reformation era, the global church largely centered the Table during worship. The purpose of gathering together was to participate in the Eucharist. We see this reality in the early church as well: "Day by day, as they spent much time together in the temple, they broke bread at home and ate their food with glad and generous hearts" (Acts 2:46).

Nevertheless, because of doctrinal evolutions since the Reformation era and individualistic syncretism, Western free-church traditions have overwhelmingly centered the pulpit while decentering the Table. The sacrament of the Word (Scripture) has been elevated over the sacrament of the Table. In other words, the sacrament of listening to God's revealed words in Scripture has replaced the sacrament of participating in God's revealed Word, Jesus, through his real presence at the Table.

Father David Harvey often tells his congregation, "You may come to church one morning and not experience Jesus in the liturgy and worship music. You may even come to church one morning and not experience Jesus through my sermon. But you will always encounter Jesus at the Table—even if you don't feel it in the moment. Because his real presence is at the Table." Why would we not want to encounter Jesus at the Table? And why would we not want others to receive Jesus at the Table?

One of the most beautiful, anti-colonial things about the Table is the way it visibly unifies all of us in Christ, regardless of socioeconomic status, race, gender, or politics. The Table is a rare place on earth where people who have nothing else in common suddenly find themselves reminded of how they hold the most important thing in common with each other, which is being united by the body and blood of Christ. The colonizer's gospel divides to conquer, but the gospel of Christ unites to heal. In a Western church that is highly divided on issues of theology, race, politics, and socioeconomics, the Table can be a physical place of healing and unification. Unless we learn to receive the body of Christ with our enemies at the Table (which requires allowing our theological and political enemies to participate at the Table with us), we will never know what it looks like to become the body of Christ for this broken world in need of healing.

If the local church is to resist the divisive ways of empire, the Eucharistic Table must become the inner sanctum from which the church draws its strength to be salt, light, and liberation for this world. And until and unless we recenter the inerrant and infallible presence of Christ at the Table while decentering the error-prone and fallible presence of the preacher at the pulpit, we will keep repeating the same abuses against marginalized communities. If the pulpit is fallible and if empires have always found ways to infiltrate it, the Table (and more specifically,

Jesus's presence at the Table) must become the focal point of the Sunday morning worship and liturgical experience.

By experiencing Jesus at the Table, we are drawn back to community in the church, however imperfect the institution is. The late Rachel Held Evans once made this observation:

> It was the sacraments that drew me back to church after I'd given up on it. When my faith had become little more than an abstraction, a set of propositions to be affirmed or denied, the tangible, tactile nature of the sacraments invited me to touch, smell, taste, hear, and see God in the stuff of everyday life again. They got God out of my head and into my hands. They reminded me that Christianity isn't meant to simply be believed; it's meant to be lived, shared, eaten, spoken, and enacted in the presence of other people. They reminded me that, try as I may, I can't be a Christian on my own. I need a community. I need the church.[5]

We get God out of our heads and into our hands when the priest or pastor or deacon hands us the elements and tells us, "The body of Christ broken for you. The blood of Christ shed for you." What better way is there to be reminded of Christ's real presence with us today?

When we recenter the Table, we're better able to persevere in Christ when human church leaders inevitably prove themselves to be mortal and fallible. I know many Jesus followers who end up walking away from the faith because they came to know Jesus through the powerful preaching gifts of their pastors, only for those pastors to end up disappointing them, as all humans ultimately do. This is especially true when the disappointment comes in the form of financial, sexual, and spiritual abuse scandals. These Christians then question if any of their ecclesial experiences of Jesus were true—understandably so, given that their experience of Jesus was primarily through the words preached from the pulpit.

When we decenter the pulpit and recenter the Table, we church leaders get out of the way, step back, and communicate to our people: "It's not about me. It's about Jesus. It's about the body of Christ broken for you. It's about the blood of Christ shed for you. Come and receive directly and freely from his real presence at the Table." This way, when we ultimately disappoint our people (hopefully not through a scandal!), they may be disappointed in us, but they *will* be confident about their encounter with Jesus at the Table.

Recentering the Table is no silver-bullet solution for all the problems of the Western church today. After all, several Eucharist-centered traditions within the Western church have directly harmed their neighbors, not least through their support of colonization. But all theology is written for a specific time and place, and I wonder if this is something that needs to be prioritized by the Western church today in order to fix our eyes on Jesus, who is the liberator who sets us all free—physically and spiritually. Still, I have to believe that a local church that deliberately centers the Table (and Jesus's presence at the Table) is going to be a constant threat to empire and its narrow, divisive, and unjust ways.

Decolonizing Western Christian Education

When we decolonize our pulpits to prioritize justice Jesus's way, it's also imperative to decolonize Western Christian education. Western Bible colleges, seminaries, and divinity schools produce thousands of church leaders each year. These leaders then lead the spiritual formation of Christian communities throughout the West.

I myself am a product of one of these Western Christian institutions. My experience at one of the West's leading conservative, evangelical seminaries was a relatively smooth one, despite a classmate or professor occasionally making the odd racially insensitive statement or assumption—nothing that Christians of color in the Western church are not accustomed to. The vast majority of my professors and administrators encouraged and championed me as a visible racial minority. They would also regularly ask for feedback on how the institution could be more inclusive of racial minorities.

But regardless of the best individual human intentions, systems and institutions in the Western church that haven't disentangled their practices from a colonizing gospel will let people of color down. For example, over the course of nearly seven years of seminary, I can think of only one South Asian theologian's book on a required reading list—and this theologian was then a professor at my school. Toward the end of my time in seminary, I did notice a more intentional effort to incorporate Global South, Black, and immigrant theologians into our curriculum. I hence find myself cautiously optimistic about the future of this particular institution. Still, most majority-culture Western church leaders have not been exposed to Global South, Black, or immigrant theologians as part of their theological training.

Anthony G. Reddie, professor of Black theology at the University of Oxford, writes on the need to decenter white male theologians as a way to decolonize Western Christian education: "When I was an undergraduate student in Church History at the University of Birmingham in the mid- to late 1980s, we spent a great deal of time looking at the writings of great luminaries such as Martin Luther, John Calvin, among others. At no point were they ever racialized—that is, ever described as 'White authors' or 'White thinkers.' These individuals were simply 'authors' or 'thinkers.' Their ideas were generic and, most importantly, they had universal implications for all peoples."[6]

Reddie goes on to assert that it is not only Western Christian education that tends to compartmentalize, otherize, and exoticize thinkers from Global South and majority world streams. He writes about his experience studying English literature in the United Kingdom, wherein an author from Africa was described as "only an African writer" whose work "shed light on a particular community and cultural reality in postmodern, post-independence Africa," instead of being something that was "generically universal." Reddie identifies this generic universalism, which has been applied to white thinkers but not to non-white or Global South thinkers, as a product of colonialism.[7]

Almost all of the required reading for my systematic theology and biblical studies classes were books written by white theologians and Bible scholars. Yet these works were never presented as "white theology," just systematic theology or biblical theology. The only class in which I was widely exposed to Black and Brown theologians was a political theology class I took with a Black professor who challenged us to read global church voices outside our comfort zones. These theologians were categorized as "liberation theologians" or "Black theologians" instead of just "theologians." This pattern of generic universalism, applied to white thinkers, theologians, and Bible scholars, is prevalent across Western Christian education, and it mirrors the experience of other non-white or Global South Christians in both conservative and progressive Western theological institutions.

Eve Parker, a lecturer in modern Christian theology at the University of Manchester, writes of Western theological institutions, "This is where Black and majority world theologies are often missing from curricula, where staff bodies are dominated by the White middle classes, and where theologies that stem from the privileged White, male elites are deemed as trustworthy knowledge, in comparison to the 'contextual theologies' that stem from the bodies of the marginalized."[8] Parker calls this a symptom of a colonial theological outlook of Christian mission shaped by colonizing empires, even going as far as labeling this an epistemic genocide or "epistemicide," which is "the killing and annihilation of systems of knowledge."[9]

Reddie shines a light on what happens when any white thinker or theologian from the protected canon of Western Christian theology is critiqued. He states, "Christian theology, often called 'The Queen of the Sciences,' has been in operation for nearly 2,000 years now, and in that time it has imbibed the invisible constructs of Whiteness to the point where attempts to deconstruct its historical edifice would lead to the complete demise of the whole enterprise."[10] Instead of blowing up the whole enterprise, Reddie recommends this unique approach to decolonizing Christian education: "My proposal for decolonizing the curriculum is the metaphorical attempt to inject Black and postcolonial perspectives into a White-dominated edifice in which the blandishments of Whiteness have held centre stage for so long."[11]

By his use of the term "whiteness," Reddie is not critiquing white people or asserting that all white people have privilege. Rather, whiteness as defined by Reddie, Willie James Jennings, and other scholars is "the epistemological underpinning of a set of theo-cultural constructs, systems and practices that govern how theology and education operate in the West and which inform our ways of being and our praxis."[12]

I share Reddie's approach to decolonizing Christian curriculum and encourage the infusion of Black and postcolonial perspectives into Christian theological education for a more robust, globally and historically informed Christian faith. Decolonizing our theology does not have to mean blowing up the entire faith, as some progressive post-evangelicals would choose to do. Nor does it need to mean ignoring the shortcomings of a corrupted faith that has been shaped by the unjust colonizer's gospel, as many white conservative evangelicals do. To decolonize our theology is to keep the essentials of the Christian faith (as taught to us by the earliest creeds of the historical global church, such as the Nicene Creed and the Apostles' Creed), while finding teachers who are closer to the margins.

A few years ago, I critiqued the eighteenth-century Western theologian Jonathan Edwards. My critique centered on his unrepentant slaveholding. My point was to encourage us to find better teachers whose theology was not tainted by their abuse or enslavement of their marginalized neighbors. The blowback was vicious. Unrepentant, unjust Christian thinkers like Edwards have been canonized within Western theological education to the point that any critique of them is perceived as a critique of the entire Christian theological enterprise. I have also experienced similar pushback from Western Christians (especially Reformed and Catholic Christians) any time I critique parts of Augustine's or Aquinas's theology.

When we decolonize our theology by infusing Black, Global South, and postcolonial teachers who did not abuse, colonize, execute, or enslave their neighbors, we will stop making excuses for our teachers who did. When we decolonize our pulpits by decolonizing the theological education of our church leaders, we will take a huge step toward recovering the just and liberating gospel of Jesus of Nazareth. And who knows? Perhaps we will also stop making excuses for our own negligence of the justice issues in our lifetime.

Deconstruction without decolonization is pointless because it does very little for our marginalized neighbors. "Decolonization," however, can be a very nebulous term. In order to demystify decolonization and contextualize it for the Western church, I provide three tangible ways the church can prioritize the justice of Jesus for our marginalized neighbors: decolonizing our budgets, decolonizing our pulpits, and decolonizing our theology. In order to embody what I'm preaching here, I try to get out of my own way by centering male and female voices from Christian communities across the global church, voices that most of us in the Western church are likely not accustomed to hearing. These include the voices of St. Thomas Christians (my own ancestors' faith tradition), Palestinian Christians, Indigenous Christians, and Black Christians, among other faithful siblings in Christ who live in close proximity to the margins. In fact, if you skip to the notes section of this book, you'll see that the vast majority of theological voices I quote in this book belong to the above categories of teachers within the global church—teachers who are also often underrepresented in Christian publishing.

These ways of decolonizing the pulpit and decolonizing Western theological education are by no means the only ways of decolonizing our theology. Much more can (and has) been written about what this could look like for the Western church. My hope is that these ideas provide a starting point for those of us who deeply love Jesus and justice for our marginalized neighbors, while finding ourselves perplexed about the way forward. It's time to usher in a new reality across the Western church—a reality that decolonizes our faith of its unjust, colonizing, and slaveholding influences—so we can re-prioritize the justice of Jesus for our marginalized neighbors.

REFLECTION QUESTIONS

1. What are some ways you can encounter Jesus to a greater degree at the Eucharistic Table? How might this strengthen your pursuit of justice?
2. If you are a church leader or an everyday Christian who influences your church community, what are some takeaways you might be able to act on from this chapter?
3. How have you experienced or heard the pulpit being colonized or co-opted by empire?
4. Who are some Christian authors, thought leaders, and voices from the margins that you can learn about Jesus from?

5

Decolonizing Our Communities

> If we believe God has engaged and continues to engage in history, we can never stay static and be happy with the status quo.
>
> —Joseph Mar Thoma, Metropolitan of the Malankara Mar Thoma Syrian Church

In 1498, Portuguese explorer Vasco da Gama arrived in Calicut, India, after months at sea trying to discover a new trade route from Europe to India. The trade route would be critical to the commercial and economic interests of the Portuguese Empire. For the Portuguese, the best way to extract South Asia's prized resources (specifically, its vast array of spices) was to subjugate local rulers and colonize India. But their effort to colonize India for the extraction of its spices was not just a political and economic endeavor; it was also a theological one.

To the Portuguese, an autonomous, centuries-old Christian tradition tracing its roots all the way back to the apostle

Thomas (one that historically preceded their own tradition), threatened colonial and trade interests. Initially, the Portuguese approached St. Thomas Christians as allies. They advocated for their rights with local Hindu rulers and assumed that the famed warrior skills of St. Thomas Christians could bolster the Portuguese military. But as they learned of the distinct theological and sacramental frameworks of St. Thomas Christians, the Portuguese became antagonistic. In due time, they came to believe that assimilating and subjugating St. Thomas Christians was key to claiming southern India's spice production regions. This was because, while the Portuguese navy controlled the coastal areas, St. Thomas Christians occupied the rich, interior land that was crucial for cultivating spices like cinnamon, cardamom, and black pepper—spices that at that time were unique to their homeland.

Portuguese clergy entered the St. Thomas Indian churches and insisted that Mass be performed according to the Latin rite (in lieu of their traditional Byzantine Syriac rite). Despite being grounded in the same ancient creeds, the St. Thomas Christians were falsely labeled Nestorian heretics, and their baptisms were declared illegitimate. Backed by the Portuguese military, Portuguese clergy wrote letters to the king of Portugal and the pope, outlining their plan to Latinize St. Thomas Christians and ultimately bring them under Rome's rule. In time, the Portuguese colonizers were given official papal authority to expand Catholicism in the East, with Goa as their ecclesiastical and missions-staging center for all of India, Japan, and China.

The Portuguese Catholics, combining military might with Jesuit demands, imposed Roman Catholic beliefs on these ancient Orthodox communities. In addition to forcing St. Thomas clergy to abandon their wives and families, they demanded that St. Thomas Christians refer to Mary as the mother of God (Theotokos) instead of as the mother of Christ. Additionally, St. Thomas Christians were now expected to venerate the saints via the use of images—something they had resisted for centuries in order to differentiate themselves from their Hindu neighbors. Portuguese authorities also proceeded to sow discord between local Hindu rulers and St. Thomas Christian communities, who had mostly enjoyed good mutual relations for centuries.

Portuguese Catholic authorities also brought Mar Abraham, archdeacon of the St. Thomas Church (its senior-most official, who served directly under the patriarch of the Syrian Orthodox Church), under papal control. They forced Abraham to sign a document disavowing Nestorianism and calling the patriarch of the Syrian Orthodox Church a heretic. Then, in 1599, the Portuguese Catholics convened a synod of St. Thomas Christians called the Synod of Diamper. This historic synod established Catholic doctrines and hierarchical ecclesiastical structures that St. Thomas Christians had to embrace. This synod in many ways completed the Western, Latinized assimilation of the St. Thomas Indian Church. The Portuguese navy also regularly intercepted vessels containing Persian and Syrian bishops sent to check in on the St. Thomas Indian Church—and sometimes imprisoning them—so as to completely sever ties between the Syrian Orthodox and St. Thomas Indian churches.[1]

If you're reading this account as a Western Christian, you might come away thinking that the Portuguese Catholic colonizers were the worst. But it wasn't just them. And it surely wasn't just Catholics. Western colonizing forces have consistently disrupted the peace among local churches in the Global South, where Christ has always been present—regardless of which empire or denomination's backing they had.

Palestinian Christian historian Mitri Raheb writes of the Protestant missionaries in Palestine (modern-day Israel) backed by the Prussian and British empires: "The (Protestant) missionaries thought of themselves as superior in religion, race, and culture to the other monotheistic religions as well as to the local churches. They often looked at them through the prism of orientalism. . . . The Protestant missionaries viewed the local Orthodox churches as 'dead.'"[2]

As an aside, Church of England missionaries in southern India are also known to have often dismissed St. Thomas Indian Christianity as "dead." During my time living in the West, I've heard many evangelicals dismiss Catholic, Orthodox, and even mainline Protestant churches as "spiritually dead" or "rote." I too was taught to see these traditions that way in my Global South evangelical upbringing. How fascinating to learn that this attitude and posture has deep colonial roots!

According to Raheb, Western Protestant missionaries found it easier to attract converts from ancient churches (such as the Coptic Egyptian Orthodox Church, the Greek Orthodox Church, or the Armenian Orthodox Church) than to find new Jewish converts—even though their original intent was to make Jewish converts. That's right. Attracting Christians from other churches (a practice common in the Western church today) also has colonial roots. Raheb also describes these Protestant missionaries (American Baptists, German Lutherans, and British Anglicans) as competing with Western Roman Catholic missionaries in the Middle East, who also intended to convert ancient Eastern Christian communities to their way of worshiping Jesus.[3]

I share all of this historical context to make this point: Western colonization has shaped Western Christianity to look down on Global South Christians and tell them, "Our way of worshiping Jesus is superior to your way of worshiping Jesus." This attitude persists today, despite the fact that Jesus has been known to these ancient communities longer than he has been known to the church in many parts of the West.

Until we examine the colonial influences hiding behind our theological postures, we will never be able to prioritize justice for our most marginalized neighbors. And in order for us to decolonize our theological postures, it is important for us to explore these ancient Christian communities to retrieve what was lost in colonization and to reimagine a new way forward for the church today, a way that reclaims justice and liberation for those whose voices have been silenced. Only when all are heard and valued equally will the gospel of Christ truly be seen as good news for people in poverty and oppression.

In my research of these ancient precolonial Christian communities in the Global South church, I discovered important characteristics that can be retrieved to help us reimagine a new way forward. Here are some of them.

Unity in Diversity

Saint Thomas Indian Christian leaders today assert that for nearly fifteen hundred years (before their Portuguese colonizers showed up), St. Thomas Christians were largely at peace with Christians from other traditions. In fact, when Persian Christians were persecuted around AD 351, St. Thomas Christians welcomingly integrated Persian Christians who fled to southern India—despite theological and cultural differences. The descendants of these Persian Christians still live at peace within the larger St. Thomas Indian Christian Church.

When St. Thomas Christians were first exposed to Portuguese Catholic clergy, they extended the same warm embrace to them that they did to other Christian traditions they had come into contact with. But soon, it became clear that to the Portuguese colonizers, the traditions of St. Peter and St. Thomas could not coexist on an equal footing. So the Eastern spiritual descendants of St. Thomas were colonized under the Western spiritual descendants of St. Peter with much of their ancient history erased with the burning of church documents at the Synod of Diamper in 1599—ancient Christian history that has been permanently erased thanks to Western colonialism. Think of all the ancient, Eastern ways of understanding and experiencing Jesus that have been permanently wiped away from human memory because of this colonizing posture of the Western church.

For the Western church to prioritize justice today, we have to become the answer to Jesus's prayer in the garden at Gethsemane, which is the same prayer that caused Jesus to sweat blood, according to Luke 22:44. Clearly, Jesus must have been praying for something that he knew would be agonizingly difficult. Here is the apostle John's detailed account of an important part of this prayer:

> I ask not only on behalf of these but also on behalf of those who believe in me through their word, that they may all be one. As you, Father, are in me and I am in you, may they also be in us, so that the world may believe that you have sent me. The glory that you have given me I have given them, so that they may be one, as we are one, I in them and you in me, that they may become completely one, so that the world may know that you have sent me and have loved them even as you have loved me. (John 17:20–23)

Did you catch that? Jesus prayed for *us*—the ones who would believe in Jesus through the word of the apostles. And even Jesus knew he was likely asking God for a lot in this prayer. If you are a Western Christian, you have likely heard this text (and, more specifically, the account of Jesus sweating blood as his prayers get more agonizing) interpreted as relating to Jesus's anxiety about his upcoming suffering. But we might also consider that Jesus's anxiety could be based on knowing how we would treat each other after he would ascend into heaven.

How many church leaders do you know who agonize over this oneness? How many churches are passionate about living in ecumenical peace with other siblings in Christ around the world who disagree with them on various things theologically?

If we're being honest, most of us (including myself) have a hard time even regularly attending church with people who think differently from us on current theological and political issues. But with the help of the Holy Spirit, peace across the larger Western church and within Western local churches is possible.

Lakeside Church in Guelph, Ontario, has been on a fascinating journey over the past few years. Once the largest church in their city, Lakeside's leaders preached through the Gospel of Luke over a span of two years during the COVID pandemic. The preaching of this Gospel account (one that uniquely emphasizes Jesus's heart for people on the margins) changed the trajectory of the church. Leaders went on to examine their posture toward the LGBTQ+ community. The church had already formed a marriage and sexuality advisory committee of both LGBTQ+ inclusive and non-inclusive church leaders (most were adherents of the traditional, non-affirming view of marriage and sexuality coming into this committee). Their deep study of Scripture, accompanied by the interpretive voices of faithful Christians on the margins, led this committee and church community to become fully inclusive of their LGBTQ+ neighbors, a decision by the elders that was formally announced to the congregation in January 2023 after several congregational town hall meetings.

Despite this decision to become fully inclusive, Lakeside leaders were eager to hold on to unity in diversity—especially toward Christians in their community who believed Scripture and church tradition don't lead to the affirming view. By adopting a posture of "deep faith, wide embrace," the pastors then went about forming another committee to update the church's statement of faith, an update that reflected their formal position.

Then, after months of prayerful discernment, pastors Marc Gagnon and Robyn Elliott unveiled Lakeside's new statement of faith to their congregation, a statement inspired by Eucharist Church, another ecumenical, Jesus-centered church in the nearby city of Hamilton. Instead of focusing on the many important issues that can divide believers (the mode of baptism, political opinions, LGBTQ+ inclusion, colonization, and so on), Lakeside has focused on uniting around the most basic, shared beliefs of the Christian faith, beliefs found in the Nicene Creed, one of the oldest creeds of the global, historical church affirmed by the overwhelming majority of Christian traditions globally. These churches include the Catholic Church, the Orthodox Church, the Anglican Church, the Mar Thoma Church, and the overwhelming majority of Protestant and evangelical churches across the world. To Lakeside Church, the Nicene Creed is the doctrinal true north.

Lakeside's new, simplified statement of faith is a model for how churches can decolonize their theology to prioritize justice for their marginalized neighbors. A faith centered on the Nicene Creed is a decolonized faith, because this was the one unifying creed throughout the global church until the Western colonizing empires and denominations started imposing their own forms of theological gatekeeping on the Global South traditions they sought to colonize. The following is from Lakeside Church's statement of faith:

> It is our commitment to Jesus that compels us to move towards others (unity). The deeper we grow in the love of Christ for us, the wider our love should extend to people who are unlike us. We call this *deep faith, wide embrace*. This will lead to all kinds of theological diversity. You're probably used to all kinds of diversity in the church (socioeconomic, political, generational, ethnic), but theological diversity may be a new one. Christians usually have a small window of tolerance for theological diversity. For us, theological diversity isn't something to be avoided but a sign of a healthy Christian community, . . . a sign that our deepening faith is leading to a wider embrace. For us, wide embrace is one of the measures of a growing, maturing disciple.[4]

Because of Lakeside Church's decolonized, ecumenical posture, even if you disagree with its stance on LGBTQ+ inclusion, you would still be welcomed as a part of the community. This posture of unity centered on the Nicene Creed is the decolonized antidote to the colonized Christian expectation that unity must always lead to uniformity.

The just and liberating gospel of Jesus of Nazareth shapes us to embrace ecumenical unity instead of divisive uniformity. This is critical for the church's pursuit of the justice of Jesus, because no one local church or denomination can singlehandedly take on a form of injustice on their own. Injustice and oppression thrive because the forces of darkness allow it to thrive. But the church, in its beautifully diverse entirety, is called to be the light in the darkness for all human flourishing. As we see in Genesis 1, light brings life.

If the forces of evil and darkness are mobilized to hinder human flourishing, then how much more should the church put aside its differences in support of human flourishing? If we believe that those who face physical violence and oppression deserve our best, we will put aside any requirement of uniformity and prioritize unity for the reduction of the injustices facing our marginalized neighbors—both locally and globally.

Today's global church can be one of the most effective forces for the good and flourishing of our marginalized neighbors around the world. As individual Christians, we can often feel helpless in the face of poverty, violence, human trafficking, and sexual exploitation. But when we mobilize our local church communities (despite different theological and political opinions within) to take action, such as in the ways we will explore together in the next section of this book, these injustices start to seem a lot less intimidating. When our churches rally together with churches of different denominations or theological persuasions, the size and scope of these injustices are reduced even further. They might even start to seem a lot more manageable.

And when the Western church bands together with the church on the margins (including the Global South church) to take action against injustice and oppression, the gates of hell will start to shake and shudder. Is it any wonder that the forces of darkness in this world continue to thrive when the Western church (and the global church) is busy with its own, ultimately meaningless, internal squabbles?

Unity in Diversity Through Pluralism

St. Thomas Indian church leaders do not just claim that their colonizers stopped their ancestors from living in unity with other Christians. They also believe Portuguese Catholics and British Anglicans kept their ancestors' communities from living in peaceful pluralism with their non-Christian neighbors.

Prior to the arrival of the Portuguese Catholics in 1499, my St. Thomas Indian ancestors largely lived at peace with their Hindu, Muslim, Jewish, and Buddhist neighbors in southern India. In fact, pluralism was par for the course for much of India before and after the Portuguese, French, Dutch, and British empires showed up. Despite the efforts of colonizing empires to "divide and conquer," and despite political sectarianism in post-independence India, pluralism and secularism remain a core value for the vast majority of Indians to this day. In fact, secularism as a value is enshrined in the Indian constitution, as the founding fathers and mothers of the country always intended it to respect its vast religious, linguistic, and cultural diversity.

We find evidence of pluralism in the St. Thomas Indian Church in much of the deliberations surrounding the Synod of Diamper, which, you might remember, was convened by Portuguese Catholic clergy in 1599 to align St. Thomas Christians with Western values. As a matter of fact, St. Thomas Christians were so pluralistic that they embodied something called "The

Law of St. Thomas." According to Mar Thoma (St. Thomas) church leader Joseph Daniel, "The Law of St. Thomas stands for the vision of openness and autonomy, customs and disciplinary norms of the Mar Thoma Christians that they nurtured in the Indian socio-cultural milieu since the time of the Apostle Thomas." The Law of St. Thomas is that "each one can be saved in one's own law and all which are right and lead men to heaven."[5] Yes, you read that right. The St. Thomas Indian Church was so pluralistic that they were practically Christian universalists until the colonizers showed up. And unlike the Mosaic law, which was rigid, the Law of St. Thomas seems to have been flexible.

Daniel explains further that "[The Law of St. Thomas] affirms the universal law of love. Christianity has a universal law of love that binds the Holy Trinity and love that binds humanity and nature. This law opens another level of unconditional love of God, for God is love."[6] This is how St. Thomas Indian Christian leaders have reconciled (and, to some degree, still reconcile) the Law of St. Thomas with their ancient, historical Christian faith. Now, this is not necessarily an endorsement of Christian universalism, which is the belief that in the last days everything will ultimately be reconciled and renewed through Christ, instead of some being condemned into eternal damnation. I do, however, find it intriguing that the Synod of Diamper outright rejected the centuries-old Law of St. Thomas as heresy. Portuguese Catholic authorities even went so far as to publicly burn many of the St. Thomas Church's historical documents, a tactic reminiscent of the modern-day Taliban.

Mitri Raheb, whom we heard from earlier, also portrays the ancient Eastern Orthodox communities of Palestine as being highly pluralistic and at peace with their Muslim and Jewish neighbors and Ottoman Muslim ruling authorities until the Western colonizers showed up in the early 1900s.[7] But here's why I share about this less-known aspect of these ancient,

Nicene Creed–adhering, non-Western Christian communities: Pluralism (a deep respect for and tolerance of other religions) is a profoundly ancient Christian value. It also happens to be a concept that has been deeply offensive to Western Christian sensibilities. And to prioritize the justice of Jesus, we must learn how to live faithfully at peace with our non-Christian neighbors in a highly pluralistic society.

In a recent conversation with Bishop Dushantha Lakshman Rodrigo of the Anglican Diocese of Colombo, Sri Lanka, he told me, "What the Western church needs to understand is that we breathe each other's religions here in the Global South." He then went on to describe how his diocese was prioritizing the work of justice and reconciliation in partnership with their Buddhist and Hindu neighbors—in a postwar context after a long civil war between Sri Lanka's Sinhalese majority and Tamil minority. The Global South church has no choice but to live and work in peaceful plurality with leaders of other faiths to prioritize the Jesus-ordained work of justice and reconciliation.

Pluralism is important for the Western church's pursuit of justice, because living in peaceful pluralism helps us cultivate humility and thereby develop the eyes to see signs of Christ's supreme and universal presence in all of humankind. Living in peaceful pluralism with our non-Christian neighbors challenges us to put aside our preconceived notions about them and their faith and to look for the ways in which Christ is already present and at work among these communities. I heard this perspective in 2025 at Lausanne's first-ever Freedom and Justice Network Gathering, when one Indian church leader remarked, "I think the Sikh community does a better job than the Indian church when it comes to disaster response and relief." Assuming a posture of humility with neighbors of other faiths allows us to humbly engage with marginalized communities and to learn from their perspectives—all so that our pursuit of justice is shaped by the voices of our neighbors on the margins (instead of our own wants and preferences).

Many Western Christians today are uncomfortable (and in many cases, even made fearful) by the idea of Christians living at peace and in the minority in a highly pluralistic society, even though this has been the reality for the vast majority of non-Western Christians around the world. Nevertheless, I believe that the collapse of Christendom in the West and Western Christians living in peaceful pluralism with their neighbors of other faiths (or no faith) will greatly benefit the Western church. These two things will ultimately shape us to break out of our Christendom bubbles, which often shape us to assume the worst about our neighbors who don't worship like us and prioritize justice for even those who are very different in creed, custom, and culture—if we humble ourselves and learn from these uncomfortable experiences.

Many American Christians today are uncomfortable living in pluralism and lacking political power, even though the church in Western contexts like Canada, Australia, and Europe already experiences these realities. In many ways, the Western Christian imagination has shaped us to only see two ideal possibilities for engagement with our Hindu, Buddhist, Muslim, and Sikh neighbors: convert or leave. Convert or be deported. Convert or "go back to where you came from." Convert or have your entire culture erased. Convert or go to hell.

Furthermore, the perceived loss of political power has pushed many white evangelical Christians (along with non-white evangelical Christians such as Hispanic and South Asian evangelicals) toward Christian nationalism, which purports that the foundations of Western governments have always been Christian and that the church must take political steps to keep it that way.[8] This leads us to the next unique characteristic from the Global South precolonial church that must be recovered.

Becoming One with Those on the Margins

Lisa Sharon Harper writes, "The entirety of Scripture was written and originally read and heard within the context of the colonized or those under threat of colonization. Every single writer of the entire Bible was a colonized person, under its threat or recently released from slavery."[9] Think about that for a second: Because of the Western church's long-standing access to political power, much of it has little to no idea what it is like to live on the margins. Yet unless we learn to identify with those on the margins, we will never be able to faithfully proclaim the fullness of the gospel. There was once a time when I looked at Christian leaders who gave up their privileges and moved to marginalized contexts as "radical." But the more I have fallen in love with Jesus, the more I have come to realize that there's nothing that radical about choosing to living on the margins. When Christians genuinely aspire to be more like Jesus, over time they will gradually find themselves moving toward the margins. Because these Christians know that this is exactly where Jesus is to be found dwelling among us.

Jesus, the Son of God and the Second Person of the Trinity, had everything. Literally everything. But he still left the comforts of heaven to come to earth and make himself nothing. He walked among us as a Brown Middle Eastern Jew who was born into a refugee family fleeing genocide. Ultimately, he died as an unjustly executed criminal of the state at the hands of corrupt government authorities. In other words, Jesus made himself nothing for our sake by subjecting himself to multiple forms of marginalization. I don't think there was anything coincidental about this. If we believe that Jesus's gospel is indeed good news for people in poverty and oppression, and if we believe that Jesus's gospel is just and liberating, we must also believe that Jesus subjecting himself to the status of a marginalized human being was no coincidence.

The apostle Paul affirms the marginalized nature of Christ in Philippians:

> Though he existed in the form of God,
>   [Jesus] did not regard equality with God
>   as something to be grasped,
> but emptied himself,
>   taking the form of a slave,
>   assuming human likeness.
> And being found in appearance as a human,
>   he humbled himself
>   and became obedient to the point of death—
>   even death on a cross. (2:6–8)

To follow Jesus, therefore, means to imitate his incarnational nature by following him to the margins. Now, before we proceed any further, I need to emphasize something. I often run into well-meaning Western Christians with a passion for justice who, because of deeply ingrained colonial values, believe that Christians who seek justice are somehow "taking Jesus to the margins with us." But Jesus is already on the margins. If anything, the question is not whether or not Jesus is on the margins; the question is whether or not we have the eyes to see him already present and at work there.

I am not saying that all of us need to sell all our possessions, even though some of us may be called to that. Neither am I saying that we all need to quit our jobs and look for vocations that allow us to encounter Jesus on the margins, even though some of us may be called to that too. I am only asking us to be open to the ways the Spirit of God, who guides the church to join Jesus at the margins, might be leading us to do the same.

After all, as David Harvey once said in conversation with me, "When Jesus said, 'Blessed are the poor,' he wasn't just saying that people who are poor will be blessed. He was also saying that people who are poor are already blessed." God is already on their side. And Jesus also once said we were either with him or against him (Matt. 12:30).

So whose side are we on?

Palestinian Evangelical Lutheran pastor Munther Isaac lamented in his 2023 Christmas sermon—while Gaza was being bombed—"If Jesus were to be born today, he would be born under the rubble in Gaza."[10] Many of us struggle with the idea of a marginalized Jesus being good news. Many of us find it difficult to stomach the idea of Jesus as a victim of empire (just as much as he is a victor against death). But to children under the rubble in Ukraine or Gaza, this marginalized Jesus is good news. To the victims of terrorism in Israel and around the world, this marginalized Jesus is good news. To people suffering from oppression under the boot of empire, the Jesus who is a victim of empire is indeed good news. To victims of human trafficking all over the world, waiting in the darkness of their captivity for hope, this Jesus is good news. Because this Jesus knows what it's like to be a victim of violence.

A Global Theology of Mutuality

The world has never been as interconnected as it is today. A pastor in Germany can meet weekly with a group of pastors in South Korea, even seeing their faces and hearing their voices in real time. We in the Western church now have the opportunity to leverage technology to allow ourselves to be profoundly shaped by the theology of our Global South siblings in Christ.

What if I told you that we can learn from the precolonized Global South church even in engaging with each other in a posture of mutual edification? The first known interaction of the St. Thomas Indian Church with a stream of the global church outside India was with the Alexandrian Church (from modern-day Egypt), when the first known head of the catechetical school in Alexandria visited India in AD 180.[11] In later centuries, the

Indian church went on to forge relationships with other Eastern branches of the global church (such as the Egyptian Church, the Persian Church, and the Syrian Antiochian Church). These ecumenical exchanges even led the St. Thomas Indian Church to voluntarily and organically alter its liturgy and theology.[12]

The Church of England's missionaries also helped reform the St. Thomas Indian Orthodox Church (the then-predominant stream of the St. Thomas Indian Church) in the early 1800s. One positive effect of this reform was the translation of the St. Thomas Syriac liturgy into the local Malayalam language (the native, everyday tongue of St. Thomas Christians), thereby bringing some of the best of Reformation rigor to this ancient Indian church. Unfortunately, given these missionaries' proximity to the British Empire, they introduced liturgical changes without the prior consent of the church's Metropolitan (head bishop).[13] The influence of the colonizing tactic of divide and conquer ultimately led to a major schism in the St. Thomas Indian Church (which was already broken into two groups, Catholic and Orthodox, because of the Portuguese Catholics' colonizing efforts).[14]

Nevertheless, the St. Thomas Indian Church's ecumenical engagement with the British missionaries in a posture of humility left a lasting impact. With the schisms also came reforms. The Mar Thoma Syrian Church (a member of the Anglican Communion today) translated the Syriac liturgy into Malayalam and removed prayers to the saints and prayers for the dead. In fact, in response to the influence of Anglican theology, one of the biggest changes to Malayalam St. Thomas liturgy was the invocation of the Holy Spirit.[15] This change in liturgy was likely the precursor to the Pentecostal movement that was birthed in the late 1800s in southern India out of the Mar Thoma church movement—a few decades before the Azusa Street Revival in the United States. As my friend David Harvey often says, "When we pray, 'Come, Holy Spirit,' the Holy Spirit always shows up."

Furthermore, the presence of Anglican missionaries allowed Dalit Christians to educate these missionaries on their plight—thereby leading them to advocate for the inclusion of Dalit Christians with Mar Thoma Christians.[16] The Global South church has historically embodied a posture of mutuality— allowing itself to be shaped by the theology of the Western church, sometimes for its benefit and other times to its detriment.

How can we in the Western church allow ourselves to be shaped by the theology of our Global South siblings? How can we sit at their feet in humility and learn from their theology of poverty, injustice, and suffering? How can we take a posture of curiosity and learn from the Global South church's experience of the liberating Spirit of God—the same Spirit that anoints Jesus to proclaim good news to people in poverty, captivity, and oppression in Luke 4?

Make no mistake: We need each other in the global church, the body of Christ here on earth, until Jesus returns. And the Western church needs the Global South church just as much as the Global South church needs the Western church. I would love to see the two embrace a more dialogical partnership in which more Western church resources are exported to the Global South church and more Global South church theology is imported into the Western church.

REFLECTION QUESTIONS

1. What are some Global South Christian traditions you're intrigued by? How can you learn more about these traditions?
2. How have you been taught to view Global South Christian traditions?

3. How can you be Jesus-centered with other Christians you don't have much else in common with? And how do you think being more Jesus-centered would allow you to better stand beside our marginalized neighbors?
4. What can we learn about the justice of Jesus from the Apostles' Creed and the Nicene Creed? How should these ancient creeds of the global church shape the way we read and teach Scripture?

6

Decolonizing Our Budgets

> Instead of the tithes which the law commanded, the Lord said to divide everything we have with the poor.
>
> —St. Irenaeus of Lyons, *Against Heresies*

This is a book about justice. But as you've probably picked up by now, this is also a book about wealth. Whether or not we are comfortable acknowledging this, there is a direct correlation between how we view money and how we view justice.

As a follower of Jesus as well as a child of colonization, I am simply unable to separate wealth and money from our passion for and commitment to the work of justice. I've learned a lot in recent years about the odd relationship between wealth and justice in much of the Western church. Every North American church leader knows of at least one church that took budgetary hits during the COVID-19 pandemic.

To be clear, these hits largely weren't because of financial difficulties or the economy. In fact, from my many conversations with North American church leaders, I get the sense that these budgetary hits were mostly on account of Christians silently or loudly leaving their churches because of their church's support for Black Lives Matter or implementation of public health mandates (such as masking, attendance limits, and vaccinations).

Any justice-oriented Christian in North America likely got to the end of 2020 wondering, "How did we get here? How did we go from being the light of the world to being the loudest opponents of the well-being of our Black, Brown, and Asian neighbors?"

I know many everyday, Jesus-loving, justice-pursuing Christians in North America who have not been able to attend church regularly since 2020 because their church fell apart over these issues. And I know many Jesus-loving, justice-pursuing pastors in North America who have not fully recovered from the trauma of watching church members they once considered family weaponize their wealth and walk away as soon as the church prioritized efforts that did not align with their political preferences.

Could it be that something is profoundly broken about the way we do church and the way we set up our individual and church budgets? After all, if the just and liberating gospel of Christ is indeed good news for people who are poor, freedom for people in captivity, and liberation for people in oppression, why do so many churches' budgets not reflect this reality?

One of the advantages of developing church partnerships on behalf of a justice organization in Canada is knowing how to view a church's expenditures by way of the Canadian Revenue Agency. I have spent hours on this agency's website, and here's what I can tell you: Regardless of church size or denomination, on average, the bulk of a Canadian church's budget (typically around 80–90 percent) goes toward administrative needs, such as staff salaries and property maintenance. Almost all of the remainder goes toward supporting mission work centered on ministering to spiritual needs.

The bottom line here is that most Canadian churches spend way more money on themselves or on spiritual evangelism than they do on justice work (if any at all)—local *or* global. If this is true for Canadian evangelical churches, I would venture to guess that this is also true for US evangelical churches.

Now here is an important caveat. As a nonprofit leader who manages staff teams, I absolutely think churches and Christian nonprofits should pay their staff well. There should be no two ways about this. There is something profoundly unhealthy about resorting to exploitative labor and employment practices in the name of Jesus. We can't be a church that opposes modern-day slavery if we don't pay our church staff well. Similarly, we can't be a church that stands against modern exploitation if we treat our volunteers as unimportant, irrelevant, overworked cogs in an ecclesial machine. So the large overhead administrative costs are understandable.

Still, here's where I would like to challenge us. Jesus said, "Where your treasure is, there your heart will be also" (Matt. 6:21). I would add, *where our money is, there our theology will be also*. It shouldn't come as a surprise that the vast majority of North American churches' mission budgets go toward evangelism rather than justice work.

Going a step farther: How are we spending our money? How much are we spending on ourselves? How much are we hoarding in real estate or stock options or savings accounts? And how much do we actually give to evangelistic missionary work compared with justice and compassion work? Now don't get me wrong. I'm not saying that we don't need to save for a rainy day. And there are plenty of Christian organizations that provide for *both* spiritual and material needs. But could it be that our inherited, colonized theology is also driving the way we manage our household budgets?

Now many of you may read this and say, "You know what, Joash? You're right. We should be giving to justice work just as much as we should be giving to evangelism." If that's you, here's where I'm going to challenge you a bit more. And you don't have to agree with me because, ultimately, my goal isn't for everyone to think exactly like me but for all of us to think more broadly. So here's my gentle suggestion: If the Western church has materially benefited from colonization and its effects, shouldn't its members give more money to justice work than to anything else? Wouldn't that be the biblically precedented, Zacchaeus-like thing to do?

My family has been Christian for nearly two thousand years now. The apostle Thomas brought the just and liberating gospel of Jesus to my ancestors. St. Thomas Christians and the Indian church are not perfect by any means. But throughout the past centuries, while maintaining our indigenous autonomy, we have been strengthened by other branches of the "one holy, catholic, and apostolic church"—including the Western church. As I've shared throughout this book, during our nearly two-thousand-year history, we St. Thomas Christians in India have enjoyed communion with many other Christian traditions, among them the Persian Church, the Antiochian Syrian Church, the Roman Catholic Church, and the Anglican Church. And we have allowed ourselves to interact with and be strengthened by these other traditions in the global church.

The church in my home country is growing today because of the Holy Spirit working in and through local leaders. I don't think we need more Western missionaries, printed Bibles, or gospel tracts. Instead, what we need is safe communities. We need stronger justice systems that are disconnected from their colonial roots, systems that can work for people who are poor instead of working primarily for the rich and the powerful. We need more accessible and affordable healthcare facilities.

But when will the Western church listen and learn to prioritize these physical needs instead of just the "soul-saving" needs it prefers to prioritize? From the perspective of someone who has served as a fundraiser with a justice nonprofit organization, I can tell you with certainty that Western Christians could do more toward the work of justice. And I can tell you with certainty that many Western Christians do not recognize the benefits (for both the givers and receivers) that can come from supporting their marginalized neighbors in physically tangible ways rather than just spiritual ways.

Centering the Voices of Our Marginalized Neighbors

I do all my intensive writing at my neighborhood South Asian chai café. If you ever meet up with me in the Toronto area, this is the café where we will likely end up. I do almost all my meetings here and have even influenced many non–South Asian friends to become regulars at this café.

Because I'm a regular, the Pakistani-origin manager of this café, Mohammad, has become a good friend. Mohammad calls me a "priest or something" because he once came across my Instagram account. So he knows I'm a "Christian religious type" Brown man, for better or for worse.

As I was writing this chapter, Mohammad came up to me with a moral dilemma that was weighing heavy on his soul.

"You're a priest or something, right? I could use your advice."

Every conversation that starts this way can only go uphill from there. So I was all in!

"How can I help, Mohammad?" I asked, expecting a deep theological question that my years of ministry and seminary training have prepared me for.

"There's a woman who comes in here every Friday and leaves a Bible in the women's washroom. I have no idea who this person is, but she comes in every week and leaves a Bible in there. This has been happening for the past few months now, and we have a stack of these Bibles sitting in our inventory."

My mouth opened as if Mohammad had just told me they were expanding their menu to include Scottish food. This was clearly not the moral dilemma I was expecting. As I tried to gather my words, Mohammad continued, "Here's what my staff team is struggling with. We are all Muslim, Hindu, or Sikh, and we want to be respectful to a religion that isn't ours. In my Muslim tradition, we can only dispose of a copy of the Holy Quran by burying it after washing all of its ink away. How do you recommend we dispose of these Bibles?"

Now, I'm sure this Christian woman meant well. Given the customer demographic of my neighborhood café, I would venture to guess that this woman, like me, is probably an Indian Christian. But her theology and missiology have been colonized. For this well-meaning sister in Christ, witnessing is not listening to the physical needs of our non-Christian neighbors. To this sister, witnessing seems to be born from a desire to expose everyday Brown people coming to enjoy a simple cup of chai at their favorite café to Christian Scripture by depositing it covertly in the restroom.

And instead of promoting Christ's just and liberating love, she ends up inconveniencing the café staff, who are uncertain as to what they should do with these Bibles. Instead of lovingly and relationally engaging with the physical, emotional, and spiritual needs of her neighbors, she ends up antagonizing them and making them feel like projects. At the Lausanne Freedom and Justice Network Gathering, transactional and antagonizing tactics like this were referred to by global evangelical church leaders as "insensitive mission."

Because I would once have celebrated insensitive mission tactics like this myself, it makes me wonder: Isn't this what we often do in the place of justice work as Western Christians? Whether it's evangelism or justice, I believe many Western Christians presume to understand the needs of our neighbors better than they understand their own needs. So instead of engaging in meaningful learning conversations with our marginalized neighbors, we assume we know what is best for them.

The Church of England's Church Mission Society (CMS) is guilty of having done this at one time with my ancestors in Kerala too. Convinced that the Syrian Orthodox liturgy was too Catholic, CMS missionaries tried to introduce Western Anglican liturgy and prayer books (such as the Book of Common Prayer) into local St. Thomas parishes across Kerala, but without the prior consent of the local bishops.[1] They even tried influencing a local St. Thomas Indian leader, Abraham Malpan, a key local reformer, to work on their behalf by offering him a full salary.[2]

Instead of sitting at the feet of our marginalized neighbors to learn from their experiences, we often approach them with cookie-cutter, one-size-fits-all "solutions," expecting that what works in our contexts will also work in theirs. And we weaponize our wealth and resources (much of which originated by unjust means, at the expense of the Global South) to bend their local leaders to our theological preferences.

Unless we learn to humble ourselves and curiously engage with our oppressed, disempowered, and marginalized neighbors, we will never liberate our theology and practices of their colonizer and slaveholder influences. Jesus of Nazareth is encountered standing with people in oppression far more often than he is found sitting with people in power.

Perhaps this lack of humility is why many Western Christians have a colonized view of the role of justice in Christian missions. Perhaps it's also why they have a difficult time supporting justice work that has no clear evangelistic outcome. Perhaps it's why some Western Christians will feed hungry people only if they attend a weekly Bible study. Perhaps it's why some Western Christians prefer to sponsor children's educational needs *only* if those children are being taught about Jesus. Perhaps it's why we sometimes hear stories of church people leaving gospel tracts instead of generous tips for working-class waitstaff who live paycheck to paycheck. Because to the colonized Christian mind, souls matter more than bodies.

A decolonized model of evangelism to people on the margins will not look past the oppressed bodies of our neighbors just to get to their souls. On the contrary, a decolonized model will see the state of our marginalized neighbors' oppressed bodies, lament at their reality with them, and then explore ways to physically liberate them from their oppression—the same way Jesus first liberated us both spiritually and physically. If our marginalized neighbors experience liberation through our care for their physical needs, they will have powerfully encountered Jesus's gospel, which is good news for the poor, recovery of sight for the blind, freedom for the oppressed, and liberty for the captive. And that, in itself, is a beautiful thing.

Parachuting Christian Radios

A dear friend of mine used to serve as the outreach pastor at one of the largest evangelical churches in Canada. He once asked to get coffee with me to vent about the theology influencing his church's budgetary decision-making.

"Joash, it's incredibly frustrating. If you ask my senior pastor if justice is as important as evangelism, he will say yes without any hesitation. But when given a choice between an evangelistic missions partner and a justice partner, he will always prioritize the evangelistic missions partner."

My friend went on to describe a decision their senior leadership team faced. "We had a $30,000 surplus in our budget that we wanted to give to a partner. We narrowed our choices down to two: Do we give this to our local and global justice partners to free children from sex trafficking? Or do we give it to a longtime missions partner that parachutes Christian radios with evangelistic programming into Europe?"

Much to my friend's dismay, the senior leadership decided to parachute Christian radios into Europe. Because if there was even a slight chance of loving some neighbors by caring for their spiritual needs, that seemed more urgent than loving oppressed neighbors by meeting their physical needs. My pastor friend went on to lament, "What young European even listens to radio programming these days?"

Now, before you come down too harshly on this church, think about what your church would do if presented with a similar budgetary decision. If you're from a Western evangelical church, chances are that your church would do the same—maybe not by parachuting radios into another country, but by supporting programs that ensure recipients hear the good news as opposed to experiencing it. Take a few moments to pause and wrestle with why they would do this and how you would feel about it.

Bible Studies Versus Legal Aid

A few years ago, I was asked to speak on a Christianity and culture panel for the Evangelical Theological Society in the United States. One of my co-panelists was Raymond Flanks, a Black brother in Christ who was exonerated by the Innocence Project after nearly thirty-nine years of incarceration for a crime he didn't commit. Raymond was being interviewed by Matthew Martens, an author, lawyer, and theologian I have immense respect for. And the panel was moderated by Glenn Kreider of Dallas Theological Seminary, one of my favorite former professors.

Over the course of his interview, Raymond shared about how many Baptist seminaries, Bible colleges, and church groups would visit and lead Bible studies with inmates in prison. He was incredibly thankful for these groups, which visited and served prisoners in obedience to Jesus's command to visit those in prison (Matt. 25:43).

During the question-and-answer time, a Black female academic in the room posed a rather poignant question: "Why did these Baptist seminaries, Bible colleges, and church groups visit to conduct Bible studies but not fight for you to be freed from your unjust life-imprisonment sentence?" Her question moved me profoundly, from simply appreciating these groups to asking deeper questions about them.

Why did these well-meaning Christians stick to verbally proclaiming the just and liberating gospel of Christ while completely looking past Raymond's need to be physically liberated from his unjust sentence? Why did these groups prioritize budgetary resources to proclaim the gospel of Christ verbally while ignoring the gospel of Christ concerned with his well-being by not also utilizing their resources to help set this innocent captive free? Were these well-intentioned Christians aware of America's broken criminal justice system? And why do so many Christian churches, institutions, and ministries prefer only to proclaim a spiritual "Jesus came to set you free from your sin" message, while ignoring Jesus's own definition of his gospel in Luke 4 as good news for people in poverty, recovery of sight for people in oppressive blindness, freedom for people in captivity, and liberation for people in the grip of persecution? While Mr. Flanks appreciated both his spiritual and physical liberation, why has the Western church mostly relegated itself to the spiritual realm while often abandoning the physical needs of creation (including liberation from oppression)?

The spiritually centered, physically deficient ways of proclaiming the gospel are the ways of the colonizer, not the ways of Jesus of Nazareth. We never see Jesus resorting to transactional and manipulative tactics with people in need of physical healing during his life and ministry. And we never see him prioritizing spiritual salvation over physical liberation. If Jesus of Nazareth offered both (and he did), then the church must get better at offering both as well.

I've been doing justice work long enough to see many Western Christians jump in and out of justice work. I've worked with several incredibly gifted and passionate Western Christians who once felt called to devote their time, skills, and careers to justice causes—only to leave a few months later because they were trained by their local churches to think that justice (although worthy) is less important than evangelism or discipleship. What a loss to our oppressed neighbors waiting in captivity for their liberation!

Perhaps you too feel passionate about the work of justice because of your faith in Jesus but have been taught that justice work is less urgent or important than the work of evangelism or discipleship. We'll never decolonize our budgets unless we first decolonize our theology of its unjust, colonial influences. And if the gospel of Christ is not good news for people in poverty or oppression, it is not really good news for any of us.

But even in this, we can learn from our Global South siblings in Christ. Raymond's story is not unlike the stories of the millions of people in the Global South who live outside the protection of the law, with very little access to justice for themselves. I have dear friends in places like Guatemala, Bolivia, Kenya, and Ghana who have trained local church leaders to walk alongside vulnerable women and children in their church communities and to help advocate for them against sexual violence and labor trafficking.

The prioritization of budgets on the part of both these Global South churches and their Western church partners in a postcolonial world is life changing. For example, in countries like El Salvador, even though 67 percent of women have experienced sexual violence, only 6 percent have reported coming forward and disclosing their abuse to local authorities.[3] One of the biggest reasons for this is the perceived inaccessibility of these justice systems by women and children in poor, vulnerable communities. After all, these justice systems were never designed with these traumatized women and children in mind. But over the past many years, the church in these Global South countries has been collectively busy at work making these justice systems more trauma informed, while also helping vulnerable women and children access these systems with the support of the local church. In early 2025, I had the joy of meeting with a few Assemblies of God leaders in La Paz, Bolivia. The Assemblies of God denomination in Bolivia is leading the charge on a "Safe Church" campaign across the Bolivian church by equipping church leaders (starting with their own denomination) to raise awareness of sexual violence against women and children, and to promptly report cases of sexual violence within their community to law enforcement.

How to Decolonize Our Budgets

Perhaps by now you are convinced that our churches, ministries, and personal budgets have been influenced by the colonizer's gospel, or you are at least wrestling with this possibility. In either instance, I would like to suggest three steps to help us decolonize our budgets, both individually and institutionally. First, we should assess where our money is going; second, we need to cultivate curiosity about what could be different; third, we must envision a new way forward.

Assessing Our Resources

If we truly believe that the truth will set us free, we must first come to terms with the truth—including the truth about our budgets. As such, our first step has to be an honest assessment of how we steward the resources we have been entrusted with.

How has the Western church historically spent its resources? How has your local church historically spent its wealth? How much of it has gone toward perpetuating injustice? And how much of it (if any at all) has directly gone toward the work of justice?

The same could be asked of your family's resources. If you come from a Western Christian family, how much of your family's current and past wealth and resources have been set aside to promote justice? Just as I became a beneficiary of colonization after moving to the West, how has your family benefited from colonization? If colonization has shaped the Western church to overprioritize spiritual mission work and underprioritize the work of justice, the way to decolonize our budgets is to balance out what has historically been underfunded.

Similarly, if the Western church has historically prioritized meeting the physical needs of its neighbors only when certain conditions have been met (such as a particular number of salvations, baptisms, Bible study attendees, etc.), the way to decolonize our budgets is to deprioritize the transactional, cheap justice that comes naturally to the Western church. It's even worth asking ourselves this uncomfortable question: How much of our spending on justice work was really justice work with a hidden agenda—in other words how much of our justice work has really been evangelistic work masquerading as justice work?

Again, I am not trying to devalue the importance of spiritual ministry (which includes intercessory prayer in addition to participating in the sacraments). I am an ordained deacon and priest in training, after all. But do we see spiritual ministry as divorced from physical liberation? And is the physical liberation of our marginalized neighbors important to us? If it was important for Jesus to attend to both, it should be important for us as well.

Cultivating Curiosity

Instead of swooping into vulnerable communities and assuming we know what's best for them, what would it look like for us to ask questions without any specific agenda?

One thing the colonial settlers in North America and the colonizing Portuguese Catholics and British CMS missionaries had in common was a predisposition to act as teachers instead of learners (a connection Willie James Jennings's *The Christian Imagination* helped me to make). Perhaps this is why so many Western evangelicals are comfortable exporting much-needed resources to the majority world but are deeply uncomfortable importing Global South theology into the West. In fact, as we covered in chapter 4, being in Western academic spaces, I picked up on a "theological supremacy" over Global South theology. This is true despite the fact that the Spirit is moving and the church is growing rapidly across the Global South. I once heard a US seminary professor (a retired Western overseas missionary himself) say, "The Global South world desperately needs our theology." I thought to myself, *Global South churches are rapidly growing, while ours are dwindling. And it's Global South immigrant Christians who are strengthening the Western church. Don't we need their theology?*

Despite being divinely qualified to teach, Jesus did not come solely to dwell among us as a teacher. He came first as a learner. He did not come assuming the posture of an earthly king, even though he was (and is) the King of kings, but as a servant to all. He did not originally come as a ruler (even though he will rule the earth when he returns) but as a baby—utterly dependent on the nurture of his earthly parents. He did not come as someone who bragged about having all the answers, even though he did (and does) have answers, but as someone who constantly asked questions.

So if Jesus came as a humble learner, what's stopping those of us in the Western church with power, influence, and affluence from taking a similar learning posture with our siblings who may have something to teach us through their unique life experiences? And how do we invest in becoming better learners who sit at the feet of our oppressed and marginalized neighbors?

Envisioning a New Way Forward

The best way to erase a bad legacy is to envision or imagine a new legacy. And given our active participation in the historical oppression of marginalized communities globally, the Western church needs desperately to envision a new way forward.

You may not have much control over what the Western church collectively does from here on out. But you probably have control over your own household budget and finances. You probably have some influence over your church community's budget. And you likely have some influence over your denomination, church network, or ministry's budget. So instead of being discouraged by everything outside our influence and control, let's do what we can with what we have.

It's nice to be successful. It's important to be effective. But God doesn't ultimately desire for us to be successful or effective. God desires for us to be faithful. If you're a part of a church, what would it look like for you to pull together like-minded people in your community, including its leaders, to envision a new, just future together? And what would it look like for your church to bring marginalized voices inside and outside your community together to envision what your church's local and global justice vision looks like?

Envisioning or imagining a just future for the Western church is difficult work. It's also costly work. But if we believe that our oppressed and marginalized neighbors deserve our very best, we will proactively decolonize our budgets to prioritize justice.

REFLECTION QUESTIONS

1. What financial resources and capital campaigns would it take to make our churches a local (and global) beacon for justice in our communities?

2. What about the way we spend our money (both individually and collectively) needs to change to usher in this new reality of decolonized budgets?
3. To usher in God's new creation, we have to part ways with the old. Even if that means drastically changing the way we steward the financial resources we find ourselves entrusted with. What are some of the old financial preferences you need (or your church needs) to let go of to make way for God's new creation?
4. Can you identify a way you have seen church or ministry budgets utilized to do "soul-salvation" work in the name of justice work?

PART 3

HOW YOUR LOCAL CHURCH CAN PRIORITIZE THE JUSTICE OF JESUS

7

Prayer

> One of the most important tasks of postcolonialism today is calling attention to the empire in our midst.
> —Anthony G. Reddie, *Deconstructing Whiteness, Empire and Mission*

You may be familiar with the phrase "land acknowledgment." Land acknowledgments, now becoming more prominent in settler colonial nations such as Canada, the United States, New Zealand, and Australia, are formal announcements at events where organizers acknowledge the original Indigenous inhabitants of the event's location. Many Canadian churches now do formal land acknowledgments as part of their services.

While land acknowledgments can be helpful, they can also be a form of virtue signaling if not backed by action. Stirling Avenue Mennonite Church in Kitchener, Ontario, is determined to go a step further than just land acknowledgments. In July

2024, this Mennonite church, built on land procured from the Six Nations Haudenosaunee Confederacy of the Grand River Territory through illicit means in the late 1800s, paid 1 percent of their annual budget ($4,000 CAD) to a Six Nations educational institution as an initial act of reparation.[1] This community allowed their land acknowledgments to shape them into meaningful action on behalf of their wronged Indigenous neighbors.

Just as some use land acknowledgments as a virtue-signaling excuse for apathy and inaction, in the same way, prayer is often treated by many Christians as an excuse for apathy and inaction. Prayer the way Jesus teaches has always been intended to shape us for action and engagement on behalf of our marginalized neighbors. Just like land acknowledgments shaped Stirling Avenue Mennonite Church to prioritize reparative action, our prayers have always been meant to shape us to be more like Jesus.

Being Formed and Transformed by the Lord's Prayer

Everything we need to understand about what prayer has to do with justice is found in the prayer that Jesus teaches us to pray, a prayer historically referred to as the Lord's Prayer. The Lord's Prayer is a terrific prayer for justice. As an advocate for justice who prays liturgical prayers each morning and evening (often via Zoom with a group of fellow clergy and oblates in my order), I find my strength to persevere in the work of justice by praying the Lord's Prayer daily. Allow me to go through this prayer with you verse by verse.

Our Father in heaven, hallowed be your name.

The Lord's Prayer starts by acknowledging our heavenly Father, who is also Jesus's heavenly Father, making Jesus our brother just as much as he is our liberator. The work of justice is ultimately the work of God, and it's a work we're called to shoulder in partnership with Jesus. Additionally, "Our Father" is not just the Father of people who follow Jesus; he is the Father of all humanity and creation, even those who do not recognize him as such. When we start prayer acknowledging that we're children of this heavenly Father, we are reminded that we are a part of a cosmic order much bigger than ourselves. We are a part of this larger cosmic reality alongside Jesus, who makes the Father known to us. And we bless the name of the Father by reminding ourselves that hallowed (or holy) is his name. A holy God finds injustice greatly unholy.

Your kingdom come, your will be done, on earth as it is in heaven.

When we pray for God's kingdom to come, we are also ultimately praying for the empires of this earth to be wiped away. This is because these two things cannot ultimately exist at the same time. Either we fight to preserve empire, or we persevere in working toward God's kingdom being fully realized on earth, as it is in heaven—a kingdom that is diametrically opposed to the empires of this earth. Praying for God's kingdom to come is also praying for the just world that God promises to realize: a world where every tear is wiped away, all oppression ceases, and God's justice is fully restored and realized. Additionally, to pray for God's kingdom to come on earth as it is in heaven is to actively pray for "the old order of things" (including the empires of this earth) to ultimately pass away. We see this vision of restoration in the book of Revelation, where John writes, "And I heard a loud voice from the throne saying, 'Look! God's dwelling place is now among the people, and he will dwell with them. They will be his people, and God himself will be with them and be their God. "He will wipe every tear from their eyes.

There will be no more death" or mourning or crying or pain, for the old order of things has passed away'" (21:3–4 NIV).

Give us this day our daily bread.

When we ask God to give us our daily bread, we are asking God to give *all* his children their daily bread. "Give us this day our daily bread" was never meant to be an individualistic prayer, as many of us are likely to hear it. Jesus taught this in a communal context, and this is as much a communal prayer as it is an individual one. World hunger is a problem that causes millions of children to suffer each year. We must look to become the answer to this prayer on behalf of others as we ask this of God for ourselves. At a time when Western governments are significantly scaling back on the reparative work of foreign-aid programs to feed malnourished children in the postcolonial Global South, this prayer also forms us to advocate for the daily bread of our vulnerable and marginalized neighbors with the powers and principalities of these Western empires.

Furthermore, in Jesus's context, where money was concentrated in the hands of the rich and powerful, everyday people in poverty (the vast majority of Jews in Jesus's time) struggled daily to provide sustenance for themselves and their families.[2] Himself a poor, colonized Palestinian Jewish man, Jesus identifies with people in poverty and oppression by encouraging all his disciples (rich and poor) to embrace a life of responsible frugality by not hoarding wealth for themselves but instead relying on the Father for their daily sustenance.

And forgive us our trespasses, as we forgive those who trespass against us.

This is where the Lord's Prayer gets real, especially for the justice seeker. In a world (and Western church) that often makes us choose between forgiveness and justice, Jesus teaches us that there is plenty of grace to go around in the kingdom of God; however, grace must never be an excuse for a lack of accountability. We cannot take this part of the Lord's Prayer out of context to excuse abuse—especially abuse in the church. A holistic view of the justice of Jesus does the hard work of envisioning a just path of restoration for perpetrators, one that includes accountability, while also protecting our marginalized neighbors. This is challenging, but God's redemptive and restorative grace invites us to do the difficult, nuanced work of facilitating restorative justice for both perpetrators and survivors.

Forgiveness is a beautiful thing, but it's often weaponized against survivors of oppression. It's not uncommon for church leaders to pressure spiritual and sexual abuse survivors to forgive those who have harmed them. The same could be said for people of color in the church, who are sometimes expected to set aside any desire for accountability and skip straight to reconciliation. But the justice of Jesus prioritizes justice for the oppressed before expecting any reconciliation. This idea is a core tenet of liberation theology and Catholic social teaching. First taught by Latin American liberation theologians such as Peruvian priest Gustavo Gutiérrez, God's preferential option for the poor emphasizes that God is first and foremost on the side of people in poverty and oppression who are taken advantage of by those with power.

Does this tenet mean that God hates the rich and the powerful? Absolutely not! But God still takes the side of people in poverty and oppression because they have no one else who can advocate on their behalf. God's preferential option for the poor is not because of the goodness of people in poverty; it is because of the goodness of God. Methodist theologian Joerg Rieger writes, "Those who are not poor are not excluded here but are invited into God's concern for the least of these."[3]

And lead us not into temptation, but deliver us from evil.

Our Western theological lenses lead us to view this line as though it is about individual sin. And when we hear "temptation," we are likely to think of sexual sin. But sin as described throughout Scripture is both individual and systemic. In addition, the Bible has far more to say about the sin of flaunting material wealth, abuse of power, and systemic oppression than it does about sexual sin.

What if we reimagined "temptation" in the Lord's Prayer to primarily be about the temptation to misuse our power? Would that help the Western church avoid its frequent spiritual and sexual abuse scandals—scandals that are ultimately about power gone wrong? Also, what does being led into temptation from a systemic perspective look like? Could it be vilifying and demonizing a certain subset of our neighbors (such as immigrants, Muslims, Sikhs, LGBTQ+ neighbors, etc.)? Could it be the temptation of unjustly excluding any subset of our marginalized neighbors from fully participating in church and society? What would it look like for your church to widen its imagination of temptation to encompass greed, racism, sexism, political power, and homophobia, among others? And what could it look like to join God in the deliverance of all of humanity and creation from the great physical evil they face in their day-to-day lives?

The justice of Jesus must have a robust, systemic view of sin and temptation, because throughout the Gospels, Jesus critiques wealth and those who unrepentantly wield it (including but not limited to the rich young ruler and tax collectors, such as Matthew and Zacchaeus) to oppress their neighbors. Jesus calls them to a better way. The same Jesus who teaches us to ask the Father to lead us not into temptation is all too familiar with the temptations of systemic oppression and the allures of empire.

Now that we have spent time closely examining the Lord's Prayer and some of its overlap with our pursuit of justice, let us embark on the work of imagining tangible things that our churches can do to prioritize prayer in a justice-oriented way.

Ways Your Church Can Prioritize Prayer in a Justice-Oriented Way

Incorporate Prayer for Justice into Your Worship Services

Prayer is never the work of just a prayer team or a prayer committee but the work of the entire church. Many church leaders want to disciple their people on complex justice issues, such as Black Lives Matter or Indigenous reparations or the Israeli-Palestinian conflict, overnight. They want to pick my brain for silver-bullet solutions on how to achieve this as quickly as possible. But discipleship is a process. And discipleship on faithful engagement with polarizing justice issues is a long-term process.

Nevertheless, prayer has the power to transform us and capture our vision as we engage in it. There's a reason why Jesus tells us to pray for our persecutors in the same breath that he teaches us to love our enemies (see Matt. 5:43–44). People who persecute us are bound to be seen as our enemies. And Jesus knows that it is impossible for us to love our enemies unless we pray for them. I don't know about you, but personally, I have found prayer for others (especially for people who have wronged me) to be deeply transformative. When I pray for people who have wronged me, I find myself fearing my enemies less. And resentment gets mystically transformed into concern. Similarly, when we pray for our marginalized neighbors, our fear and apathy gradually transforms into love and empathy. Eventually, it is this intentional prayerful posture toward our marginalized neighbors that will ultimately lead to action on their behalf.

Olivet Baptist Church in New Westminster, British Columbia, pauses during one of its services each month to fervently pray for each of its justice partners. Because of its posture of regular, intentional prayer, this small community has given over half a million dollars to its justice partners over just a few years. Prayer for our marginalized neighbors as a united church community can do wonders for our engagement in the work of justice.

What would it look like for your church to set aside time once or twice a month during worship services to intentionally pray for our poor and oppressed neighbors? What might a spiritual practice like this, embedded in the liturgy of your church, do within the hearts of people in your community? And what might your intentional pursuit of prayer on behalf of your marginalized neighbors unleash in the world?

Pray About Local and Global Justice Issues with Other Churches

Prayer isn't something meant to be done solely as an individual church community; it's also meant to be something done in partnership with other local church communities—especially those outside of our own denominational and theological boundaries. Nothing strengthens the people of God more than pursuing justice cooperatively. Working together toward a common goal allows us to focus on what unites us rather than what divides us. Praying communally for justice is important; however, this should only be an initial step.

The ultimate goal must always be praying hand in hand with other churches in your city or town, even if you cannot agree on much else theologically. There's something inexplicably powerful about Christians who may not see eye to eye banding together to take on issues of injustice. No *one* church has all the resources needed to bring an end to injustices locally and globally. It's going to take all of us coming together and pooling our resources to make a meaningful dent on problems ingrained in our societies.

One aspect of mobilizing and resourcing churches to prioritize justice that I have truly enjoyed this past decade is watching leaders and members from significantly different streams of the faith unite around something they can all agree on—the importance of addressing an injustice locally and globally. Nothing gives me more joy than watching the pastor of a liberal Methodist church and the pastor of a conservative Baptist church coming together to pray at an anti-trafficking prayer event. Or seeing a Catholic priest, a female Presbyterian pastor, and an Egyptian Orthodox bishop praying for the end of the housing crisis in their city. Doing the work of justice firsthand has exposed me to beautiful moments like this.

Praying together binds our hearts as one through the Holy Spirit and helps us realize how much we have in common with each other as siblings of Jesus and children of God the Father. If we are a church that is serious about ending injustices in our lifetime, we must put aside our distrust of other Christians and band together, starting with prayer.

Of all the things you might do in justice work, bringing together Christians from significantly different churches will likely be the most difficult. I'll even put it this way: If you are curious about what actual demonic opposition to the work of justice can look like, just try putting together an ecumenical, multidenominational prayer meeting for ending specific injustices locally and globally. Because if there are two things that upset the powers and principalities of darkness, it is Christians putting aside their differences to come together and Christians putting aside their differences to resist evil injustices.

I remember trying to organize something like this as an enthusiastic teenager in Mumbai. After meeting with the leaders of four churches (all parents of my friends), things looked really promising. The idea was simple: Bring together the youth of these churches to gather and pray once a month for justice needs in our city. But before we could even get things off the ground, two of the four churches backed out. One church that was averse to charismatic gifts of the Spirit backed out because they didn't want the Pentecostal youths in the group "corrupting" their own youths' theology. Another church backed out because they did not have a youth program and feared that one of the other churches would steal their members. This church somehow even managed to start their own youth program overnight—something I still take credit for.

If you are a churchgoer, what would it look like for you to come alongside your church leaders in putting together an ecumenical prayer gathering for justice? If you are a church leader, how can you leverage your connections with other church leaders in town to organize something like this? Are there any local or global justice organizations you can partner with regarding events like this, organizations that can be relied on to provide urgent and specific prayer requests (in addition to promoting the event within their networks)? What leaders from your own denomination and others could you invite to something like this?

Pray as a Church for Elected Leaders (on Behalf of Marginalized Neighbors)

I want to be clear as I encourage us to pray for our elected leaders: I am not encouraging us to give the pulpit to our elected leaders. Neither am I encouraging us to pray for our elected leaders in a partisan way, because the kingdom of God will always transcend partisan politics.

Instead, I'd like us to consider praying for our elected leaders on behalf of our marginalized neighbors. The reality is that in representative democracies, elected leaders have the power to shape policies that impact our marginalized neighbors. For example, when I worked for elected state legislators in the United

States as a political adviser, my clients (many of them Christian men) would often support legislation to cut food stamps for single mothers or eliminate tax credits for environmentally friendly electric vehicles, both of which are policies that have adverse effects on our marginalized neighbors—either directly or indirectly. At the same time, these politicians often supported legislation that made cannabis oil accessible to our disabled neighbors and made adoption easier for children in the foster care system, which are policies that are good for our marginalized neighbors. Through all this, these elected officials would often connect with church leaders in their districts, asking them to keep them in their prayers.

One reason I will likely never seek elected office is that I have intimately seen how difficult elected officials' jobs are. I have seen dozens of well-meaning, justice-oriented, and Jesus-loving men and women step into elected office for all the right reasons, only to lose their way a few years in by compromising their integrity and, often, the interests of their marginalized neighbors, in order to keep and grow their positions of power. These decisions are often made with the best of intentions, usually along the lines of "If I make this small compromise now, I will have more political influence to serve my marginalized constituents better long-term." But they're still compromises, and marginalized people frequently continue to suffer without hope for justice and liberation in both the near- or long-term.

The more I have studied the history of global colonization, the more I have come to see how our own Western institutions (including governments) are often shaped by empire. In addition, I have more grace and empathy for these elected leaders, whom I once judged harshly for compromising the way of Jesus for the way of empire. The way of empire really is that formidable. And our elected officials and government leaders (both Christian and non-Christian alike) need divine, supernatural strength and wisdom to resist the allure of empire to stand with all our marginalized neighbors. This is where prayer comes in.

Imagine taking time during your services to pause and pray for your elected leaders: not for their political success or for their reelection but for their well-being, for their conviction to prioritize our marginalized neighbors, and for courage to do what is right for people in poverty and oppression, despite the personal and political costs. If we can pray with intentionality for our government leaders of all parties by name and for specific policy issues affecting our marginalized neighbors, even better!

Now, perhaps you're reading all this and you're wondering, "Joash, I get how we can pray for our elected officials on behalf of our local marginalized neighbors, but how do we pray for our marginalized neighbors in other countries?" As someone who has worked as an international human rights advocacy leader, I can tell you for a fact that our marginalized neighbors in other countries deserve to be prayed for just as much as our locally marginalized neighbors. If communities in other parts of the world have historically been marginalized because of the colonial-era atrocities committed by Western government institutions (with the blessings of the Western church), we need to pray for our government leaders to prioritize them all the more.

For example, our government leaders are often confronted with opportunities to fund humanitarian and development aid in other countries, both for short-term humanitarian crisis needs and for long-term sustainable development work. It's not uncommon for government leaders to struggle to understand why these humanitarian and development aid funds should continue to be prioritized—especially because those who benefit the most from them are so far away. As Christians who want to love our marginalized neighbors well in a postcolonial world, it is imperative for us to pray for our elected leaders to continue prioritizing these funds.

After you pray for your government leaders, perhaps even consider reaching out to their offices to ask them to use their influence and power to stand with our marginalized neighbors the way Jesus stands with them. Imagine how differently elected officials and government leaders would see the church if we did this. Perhaps they would begin to see their constituents within the church not as pawns to be taken advantage of during election cycles but as formidable and consistent voices on behalf of oppressed and marginalized communities, in both election and nonelection years.

Imagine also how formative this kind of sustained prayer for our elected officials and our marginalized neighbors can be for your church community! In a day and age when prayer has often been weaponized by political leaders as a means of political propaganda, what would it look like for us to redeem prayer for one of its original purposes, which is aligning our lives with the kingdom of God?

Pray with Marginalized Communities

As we've explored already, one of the marks of colonizer theology is presuming to know what our marginalized neighbors need better than they know themselves. This comes from the colonial posture of wanting to be teachers instead of becoming humble and curious learners. If we are not careful, we can do this with our prayers for our marginalized neighbors too.

Many of us have prayed *for* our poor, oppressed, and marginalized neighbors, but how many of us have actually prayed *with* our poor, oppressed, and marginalized neighbors? There's a difference between praying *for* a neighbor and praying *with* a neighbor. Praying for someone can be unilateral and done from a posture of superiority.

When I studied at university, I lived in an under-resourced part of downtown Atlanta next door to many unhoused people. Over time, I developed meaningful friendships with many of the unhoused men in my neighborhood. On one occasion, I was invited to do a prayer walk for our unhoused neighbors with a group of students who drove in from a Bible College a few hours north. We were a group of ten that went from block to block, praying at a distance. The only interactions we had with these individuals were with those who asked for money or a meal.

Contrast this with another experience I had with a group of brothers from the campus ministry I was a part of. We went to a nearby park that was full of unhoused men with the aim of building relationships with them. We also brought them home-cooked meals to share. I'll never forget the reaction of the unhoused neighbor I handed my Indian-style masala egg omelet to. He reacted to it like someone had just offered him luxurious caviar. Amid these relationship-building conversations over food, we mentioned our faith to these neighbors and asked if and how we could be praying for them. What followed was beautiful because we did not just end up praying for them; we ended up praying with them—particularly the ones who identified as Christian. And I don't just say we prayed with them because we physically stayed with them while praying for them. In fact, it would be more accurate to say we prayed *with* them because after we prayed for these neighbors, they prayed for us.

When we pray with instead of for our marginalized neighbors, we level the playing field and see them as peers instead of "charity projects." And we treat them as equal image-bearers of God in Christ. It goes without saying that it is much easier to pray for a marginalized neighbor than with a marginalized neighbor, especially as the majority are not likely to share our Christian faith. Still, we must seek to pray with these neighbors. One way to do this is by finding Christians who live in proximity to those on the margins and who can act as intermediaries.

For example, it's unreasonable to travel to active war zones in order to pray with children being bombed to death. In such instances, we can pray with pastors from communities that are adjacent to these children. Similarly, it would not be trauma informed to try to pray with survivors of sexual abuse (unless they share our Christian faith and explicitly ask to do this with us); nevertheless, we can pray with Christians working closely with survivors.

What would it look like for our churches to pray not just *for* our marginalized neighbors but also *with* them? What would it look like for us to honor the agency of these neighbors by asking them to tell us how we can pray for them instead of condescendingly presuming to know their prayer needs? And in what ways can we leverage technology to catalyze prayer support for our marginalized neighbors and those working to serve them on the front lines?

In a world where "sending thoughts and prayers" has become an excuse for inaction, we must redemptively engage in prayer for our marginalized neighbors. Prayer has always been meant to form us for action and engagement in the work of justice—not action for the sake of action, but action that reflects the heart of God. As we see in the Lord's Prayer (the prayer Jesus teaches us to pray), prayer has always been meant to be formative. When we authentically pray for our marginalized neighbors, we align our lives with the just and liberating kingdom of God. And when our hearts are aligned with the heart of God for our marginalized neighbors, we will find ourselves caring deeply for these neighbors with our actions.

REFLECTION QUESTIONS

1. How has prayer shaped the way you have lived your life in the past?
2. How can you be more intentional with your prayers so that they shape you to become more like Jesus in prioritizing justice for your marginalized neighbors?

3. What are some ways in which you can pray for your elected leaders and government leaders on behalf of your neighbors on the margins?
4. What is one thing you can do to foster a spirit of ecumenism in praying for justice with Christian siblings across denominational lines?

8

Advocacy

> What is needed is not so much contemplation as effective action for liberation. The Crucified needs to be raised to life. We are on the side of the poor only when we struggle alongside them against the poverty that has been unjustly created and forced on them.
>
> —Leonardo Boff and Clodovis Boff,
> *Introducing Liberation Theology*

"I guess I better support this," the congressman said. He was a rural Georgia Republican member of the US House of Representatives. These were the sweetest words my group could have hoped to hear.

I was working alongside a group of anti-trafficking advocates during an advocacy day at the US Capitol. My job was to steer this passionate group of everyday Christians and church leaders from meeting to meeting. I took them from one end of Capitol Hill to another as they petitioned their members of

Congress to support legislation that would increase funds for anti-violence efforts on behalf of women and children in the civil society sector of Central America (specifically Guatemala, El Salvador, and Honduras). In advocacy meetings like this, the advocates are the heroes. My job as their advocacy leader was just to make sure we were staying on message and on time so we could make it to our meetings with other members of Congress who represented them in Washington, DC.

For this particular meeting, the congressman refused to start the meeting without our lead advocate, Christine Watson, who was from his congressional district. He had gotten to know Christine on a first-name basis because of her advocacy with his office. Christine, however, was running a few minutes behind due to another meeting.

"Where's Christine?" the congressman asked. "We cannot start this meeting without her," he said seriously.

"Yes sir, you are absolutely correct," was all I could muster. I was somewhat in awe of both the influence and the relationship that Christine had built with this congressman.

When Christine arrived, the congressman was eager to hear why she would fly all the way from Georgia to Washington, DC. After laying out the specifics of what we were asking him to support, Christine said, "Congressman, we are asking you stand with these brave women and children who have survived great sexual violence, so that no child in Central America has to endure what they have endured. This is personal to me. I have met some of these brave children in Guatemala firsthand. We need you to support this bill." Christine also came equipped with a list of pastors and faith leaders in his district and across Georgia who had signed a "faith leader letter" in support of the bill. The congressman was clearly accustomed to this kind of professional advocacy from Christine. Still, it was fun to watch his eyes pop as he saw the impressive cross-denominational list of pastors Christine and other advocates had managed to mobilize.

Even to someone like Christine, who had built trust and credibility with this member of Congress for many years, the man's response was beyond her wildest expectations—especially considering this was her first "yes" from this congressional office after years of hearing "no." But in hindsight, for Christine, even a no would have been a huge step up from what she had grown accustomed to in her early years as an advocate, which was a refusal to grant a meeting in the first place. Christine's successful faith-fueled advocacy on behalf of our marginalized neighbors is just one example of dozens of advocacy success stories I could share.

Christine is one among hundreds of everyday Christians who advocate on behalf of their marginalized neighbors with their elected leaders at all levels of government. While some Christian advocates get to visit their nation's capital to meet with elected officials, others engage in more local forms of advocacy, such as call-in days, tweet-a-thons, petitions, and more.

I've had the joy of serving as an advocacy leader in the international human rights space in three countries. I have a master's degree in political advocacy from the top political-management graduate program in the United States. Still, by no means do I consider myself an advocacy expert, because every advocacy context and every political moment is unique. There are also people and communities who are incredibly more qualified than I am to write about Christian advocacy in the public square. Nevertheless, I'd like to share several "pro tips" on Christian advocacy that I have learned from some of the best Christian advocates and advocacy leaders around the world this past decade.

It's All About Who *and* What You Know

The political world is a deeply relational world. When I worked as a campaign consultant and lobbyist, I'd often hear others in the industry say, "What you know is important, but at the end of the day, it's all about *who* you know."

I would argue that both what you know and who you know are important in advocacy. *Who you know* will absolutely get you in the door for a meeting; nevertheless, *what you know* will help others take you seriously once you get that meeting. So read up on the issues affecting the neighbors you are advocating for.

One of the advantages of doing advocacy with Christian and non-Christian organizations is that you will be trained and equipped in "the what" to represent a cause (and even an organization) sufficiently well. Still, you are likely not going to become an expert on the relevant subject matter overnight. So if you ever walk into a meeting and a government official asks you a question you don't feel equipped to answer, it's perfectly acceptable to say, "I'll have to double-check on that. Can I get back to you?" In fact, it's even advisable to be honest about your limitations and to ask if you can circle back later. Let me give you two very good reasons for admitting when you don't know something. First, it gives you an excuse to follow up and stay on the leader's radar (something you absolutely want to do as an effective advocate). Second, if you come across as someone who lies just to appear smart, government officials might see through that and then question your credibility. For lobbyists and advocates, credibility is all we ultimately have. And people in poverty and oppression deserve the most professional and credible representation in the highest halls of power.

But who you know matters just as much as (if not more than) what you know. This is because it's who you know that will get you a meeting in the first place. Now, getting to know the right people can seem incredibly difficult to a new advocate. However, since I'm writing to the Western church, and since the West is largely comprised of representative democracies, finding who you need to know may not be as difficult as you might think.

A simple Google search for your elected officials (along with your residential address) can help you narrow down the names of your elected officials and the right contact information for their offices. Once you find their contact information, give their office a phone call to introduce yourself as a constituent and to ask about the best way to schedule a meeting. Most Western elected officials even have a meeting request form on their website to make them more accessible to their constituents. And once you send in your meeting request form, be sure to call their office every other day to follow up on its status, because government offices are often inundated with meeting and event requests. These meetings can take place in their capital offices as well as their district, riding, or constituency offices.

Remember, you do not want to schedule this first meeting without having a specific policy request or having some basic knowledge about the issue you are advocating for. If you don't walk into this meeting with credibility, you'll likely not be granted a second one. As I have mentioned before, this is where it can be advantageous for your local church to join forces with nonprofit organizations working on local or global justice issues that also do political advocacy, as these organizations usually hire seasoned advocacy leaders and organizers like myself to recruit, train, and guide their advocates. These nonprofit organizations also often have the credibility needed to get you that first (and second) meeting.

Here's something else we should keep in mind as advocates of justice Jesus's way: Even though the elected officials and government leaders we interact with are ultimately representatives of an empire, they are first and foremost fellow image-bearers of God. It is important that we treat them as fellow image-bearers. It is also important that we treat them with the respect and dignity their position in government affords them, just as Romans 13 encourages us to do. When we advocate for our marginalized neighbors, we stand in the historical prophetic tradition of the church (one often neglected in the present Western church) as people of God tasked with speaking truth to power on behalf of our marginalized neighbors.

Persistence Pays Off

There are no overnight wins in justice advocacy work. Because we seek to topple the old order of things to make way for God's new creation, we are met with resistance. And effectively undoing and replacing systems of the old order of things, which oppress our marginalized neighbors, *will* take both time and patience. In a world that seeks instant gratification and quick results, the long-haul work of advocacy for our marginalized neighbors is countercultural. Still, persistence on their behalf is the way of Jesus.

The most impactful justice work is always "long-haul" work. Black civil rights advocacy efforts in the United States spanned several decades, outlasting numerous advocacy leaders and presidents—from Franklin Roosevelt and John F. Kennedy to Lyndon Johnson and Richard Nixon. In many ways, the Black civil rights struggle persists in the form of advocacy against police brutality, mass incarceration, and death penalties. This movement didn't start with Martin Luther King Jr., and it certainly didn't end with his assassination. King's legacy as a Christian pursuing advocacy Jesus's way still lives on today.

I have to embody this "long obedience in the same direction" mindset with any justice advocacy issue I take the lead on. Advocacy campaign efforts are multiyear commitments, and Christians who are serious about making impactful systemic change must be willing to commit the time, resources, and effort needed to move the proverbial needle of justice.

For example, it takes months and specialized skills to do effective policy research. Once the research is complete, political power-mapping—the process of mapping out which institutions, coalitions, networks, and relationships to leverage for your advocacy campaign—also takes months to finish. Recruiting and training your grassroots (i.e., everyday citizen advocates) and grasstops (i.e., national and regional advocacy influencers, such as faith leaders, union leaders, business leaders, and retired elected officials) takes additional time. Only after you have your advocacy infrastructure together can you finally start running your advocacy campaign at full-steam via grassroots lobbying, grasstops lobbying, and direct lobbying (meeting one-on-one with lawmakers and bureaucrats). Simultaneously, you will also likely want to run a digital advocacy campaign, in which you invite the general public to sign online letters and petitions written to their elected representatives. These grassroots, grasstops, and direct lobbying efforts can often take years to yield results and successfully move the needle by effecting policy change that benefits our marginalized neighbors.

Throughout the past decade, I have been involved in anti-trafficking and anti-violence advocacy campaigns in South Asia, Canada, and the United States. From conception to outcome, these campaigns have taken several years to materialize. If you're wondering how I've been able to do all this in ten years, it's because I inherited some of these advocacy efforts, I launched advocacy efforts that other capable leaders took on and brought to completion, and I carried other advocacy efforts across the finish line. The reality is that most advocates rarely get to be a part of advocacy campaigns from start to finish; we step in where we can and try to be faithful there. But Christians who faithfully and consistently engage in the work of advocacy over a sustained period of time will frequently find their minds blown by what God can do in and through them as partners in making all things new.

Be Politically Agnostic

One of the dangers of advocacy in the nonprofit space is the ever-present risk of having our cause be co-opted by a political party or politician for their purposes. Examples of this in the United States include the pro-life issue (politically co-opted by the Republican Party) and the LGBTQ+ rights issue (politically co-opted by the Democratic Party). Notice how I don't use the word "movement" here to describe these issues, because movements transcend political parties, and the support efforts for both of these issues are highly partisan.

When advocacy issues are monopolized by just one political side, they lose credibility as issues that transcend partisan boundaries. These issues are then denounced wholeheartedly by the opponents of the political party championing them, which is rather unfortunate, as our marginalized neighbors deserve movements that transcend partisan lines. When justice advocacy gets politicized, our marginalized neighbors are the ones who suffer.

I've been doing anti-trafficking advocacy long enough to remember the days when human trafficking was the rare nonpartisan issue. To some degree, this is still the case. Unfortunately, human trafficking has become increasingly partisan, especially with the emergence of conspiracy theories such as QAnon. In cases like this, Christian advocates for justice can't do much apart from faithfully educating elected officials and the general public with accurate information about their issue. After all, even the most devout Jesus followers who advocate for justice in the public square have very little control over things such as the political climate of a nation. In situations like this, we must set aside our desire for success (in this case, transforming the entire political climate of a nation) and prioritize faithfulness (doing what we can with what we have), even if this means we have to operate from the margins.

That being said, Christians can still do a lot to keep their advocacy issues from becoming partisan or co-opted by a political side. A helpful place to start is adopting an agnostic approach toward any party or leader. Political leaders often look for issues they can champion to make them popular with voters and keep winning elections. This can be incredibly helpful in the work of advocacy, and we must find ways to partner with such leaders while still maintaining our political independence in the public square.

Our goal as Christians must never be to reelect specific politicians; our goal should always be to faithfully advocate for our neighbors on the margins—regardless of which party or politician is in power. It shouldn't matter how supportive a specific politician is of our advocacy issues, because at the end of the day, they're always going to be imperfect advocates for our marginalized neighbors. Inevitably, because of their ultimate allegiance to their empire, they will take stances that work against our neighbors' well-being. Our marginalized neighbors are thus always best served when their justice issues are perceived as bipartisan or multi-partisan issues that any government leader can stand behind.

Christians cannot be seen as being preferential toward particular political parties or politicians because ultimately, as we explored with God's "preferential option for the poor" in the previous chapter, God *actively* sides with people in oppression. Political leaders have loved to claim that God is on their side. For example, during the Civil War, leaders of both the Union states and the Confederate states claimed that God was on their side. But the only "side" God takes is that of those whose voices are silenced. And if the oppressed and oppressor ever switch sides, God will realign with the powerless and the dispossessed. So political leaders are either with God or against God, depending on whether they are working for or against the interests of those on the margins.

A rule of thumb for Christians who wish to advocate in a nonpartisan way is to refuse to introduce a campaign or policy initiative until and unless they are able to recruit a politically diverse, cross-partisan bench of elected leaders to champion their cause. This takes time and can sometimes feel impossible, but believe me when I tell you that you'll be thankful for that broad, multi-partisan coalition in the long haul. As a Global South Christian advocacy leader once wisely shared with me during a meal, "It doesn't really matter who is in power in our country. Today it might be the right-wing, anti-Christian nationalists; tomorrow, it might be the left-wing communists. Our priorities will never change because we're called to prophetically speak up on behalf of people in oppression, regardless of who is in power."

Refuse to Get Co-Opted by Empire

We must also constantly remind ourselves that we advocate in order to pursue a kingdom that is *in* this world but not *of* this world. The just and liberating gospel of Jesus is deeply political; it's about a king and his already-but-not-yet, just, and liberating kingdom. But the politics of Jesus and his kingdom will always stand in strong contrast to the unjust and oppressive politics of the empires of the earth.

Justice Jesus's way resists the temptations of political power, which is an allure of empire. After all, Jesus came not to amass power but to give power away in order to lift those on the margins so that they may have fullness of life. He came not to be served but to serve. Therefore, any form of advocacy in the public square that claims the name of Christ while looking nothing like Jesus (such as the medieval-era crusades or today's Christian nationalism) has no place in Christian advocacy.

The justice of Jesus also resists the allures of violence, which is another way that empire tries to mete out justice. Violence seems like such an easy way to "get stuff done for Jesus." But when we resort to violence, we lose sight of God's plan for humanity and compromise Jesus's way. Jesus, who had every reason and right to choose violence, steadfastly resisted it—even when tempted by Satan in the wilderness. We, the church, must do the same. Nevertheless, quite tragically, the Western church has historically struggled with renouncing violence in service of Christ. From the crusades to colonialism, the church has often supported rather than challenged state violence. This makes it all the more important for us as Western Christians to raise our voices in peaceful, nonviolent resistance whenever empire resorts to the ways of empire. In so doing, we stand in the long prophetic line of advocates seeking justice Jesus's way (and often paying the cost for just discipleship).

Jesus called us to be the salt, light, and liberation of this earth with him. If we lose our saltiness by being co-opted by the empires of this earth and their unjust, oppressive ways, what good are we? Jesus himself said that if we lost our saltiness, our existence as the church—as Christ's body on earth—would be pointless, as we'd only be good for being trampled underfoot. If Satan tempted Jesus in the wilderness, the empires of this earth (as instruments of Satan) will also tempt Jesus's body, the church, and distract us from our task of being salt, light, and liberation while we await his return. And the empires of this earth will also tempt the church to neglect our task of fully and faithfully proclaiming the justice of Jesus.

If you are a Christian connected to a local body of believers, what would it look like for your church community to resist the allures of empire? If you are a church leader, what would it look like for you to regularly disciple your community in spotting the signs of empire so that they can resist its temptations and promote the justice of Jesus and his just kingdom? Jemar Tisby points out, "History demonstrates that racism never goes away; it just adapts."[1] Similarly, empires and their unjust, oppressive ways will never really go away; they will only constantly evolve.

Prioritize Faithfulness over Success

The Jesus way of seeking justice prioritizes faithfulness over success, and it grates against our Western, capitalistic sensibilities. Now, if you're anything like me, you also love winning. But when I find myself wanting to win at all costs, I have to pause and remind myself that contrary to my deeply ingrained passion for success (and accompanying fear of failure), Jesus does not call us to success. Neither does he call us to either capitalism or Marxism. He calls us to faithfulness.

If we prioritize success, we will compromise Jesus's way. But if we prioritize faithfulness, we will put our best foot forward and leave the final outcome of our efforts to God.

The church in the Global South has a lot to teach us on this front, as many Christians there have zero political access or influence. Marwan Aboul-Zelof is the lead pastor of City Bible Church, a hundred-person multiethnic church in Beirut, Lebanon. On August 4, 2020, a powerful explosion in Beirut killed more than two hundred people while injuring more than six thousand.[2]

City Bible Church had the church building closest to the explosion, and it was utterly destroyed in the blast. Sharing his reflections soon afterward, Pastor Marwan wrote, "It's difficult for me to express what's happening in my heart and mind. There's an overwhelming sense of God's presence right now, though I mostly have questions and few answers."[3] When I connected with Marwan virtually in August 2024, exactly four years after the explosion, he told me, "We still have more questions than answers. We're still waiting for justice in this lifetime. But we don't feel helpless because we know that even though we will likely not see true justice in this lifetime, we will see perfect justice being done one day when Jesus returns to rule the earth. We will keep being faithful until that day."

I find this attitude of City Bible Church to be deeply inspiring. Just like much of the Global South church, they will likely not experience justice on this side of eternity. But that does not stop them from being faithful by proclaiming the gospel both spiritually and physically in their ministry context with whatever resources they have. City Bible Church does what it can with what it has for its poor and oppressed neighbors—whether that's by serving war-torn refugees or by making room for voices from marginalized communities in its pulpit.

What stands out to me about City Bible Church is that they choose to prioritize the well-being of their neighbors who are even more marginalized and oppressed than they are. In Contrast with a Western world obsessed with advocating for *my* rights and *our* rights, Global South churches like City Bible focus on the rights of neighbors more than their own rights.

Even though advocacy success is an ideal, the goal for the church is never success because there is so much ultimately outside our power and control. The goal is faithful advocacy with our "everything" because we serve a good and just King of kings who deeply delights in surprising us with what's possible.

Your church will likely never end homelessness, human trafficking, or world hunger. The larger global church will likely never end these injustices once and for all. But we can and must be faithful with the resources God has entrusted to us, even if we don't succeed in ending these injustices on a large scale. Justice Jesus's way is about partnering with God to faithfully proclaim the fullness of his just gospel to people in poverty and oppression. Success is the currency of capitalistic man-made kingdoms; faithfulness is the currency of the self-sacrificing kingdom of God. And our advocacy must reflect this currency, this driving value.

I hope this chapter has helped demystify the "how" of Christian advocacy at least a bit. Christians have the prophetic task of speaking truth to power on behalf of people in oppression. This is indeed a God-ordained task of the local and global church, a means of fully proclaiming the just and liberating gospel of Christ.

If the gospel is indeed good news for people in poverty, captivity, and oppression, our local churches must engage in the work of advocacy—changing sinful, broken societal structures that hinder life for our vulnerable neighbors on the margins. If the gospel is indeed "recovery of sight for the blind in the dungeons of captivity" (as Canadian theologian Nikayla Reize says),[4] Christians and churches must prioritize the work of advocacy to allow the light of the gospel (a light that ultimately brings life) to shine on people in poverty and oppression.

The gospel or good news isn't just that Jesus came to die for the sins of the world; it's also that he is coming back to redeem and restore everything that has been broken by sin—including the sin of injustice. When we advocate for the human flourishing of our marginalized neighbors, we proclaim the gospel amid the brokenness of their living situations, both in the already (where justice is imperfect) and in the not yet (where justice is perfect and complete).

Like any kind of kingdom and gospel proclamation work, advocacy is long-term work that requires foresight, patience, and endurance over the long haul. There are no quick, overnight wins in Christian advocacy because toppling the old, oppressive order of things to make way for God's new creation takes time and resilience.

Finally, the *way* we seek justice matters just as much as *who* we seek justice for. And if our pursuit of justice or advocacy looks nothing like Jesus and his nonviolent, others-centered, just, and liberating gospel, our "Christian" advocacy is anything but Christian.

REFLECTION QUESTIONS

1. How can your church or faith community build relationships with the elected officials you hope to engage on behalf of your marginalized neighbors?
2. What are one or two justice issues that you are most passionate about becoming an advocate for?
3. How can you equip yourself to become a better advocate for the marginalized communities you hope to advocate for?
4. What is one organization you can volunteer with to build some experience as an advocate?

9

Partnership

Christ has no body on earth but yours. Yours are the eyes with which he looks compassionately on this world. Yours are the feet with which he walks to do good. Yours are the hands with which he blesses all the world. Christ has no body now on earth but yours!

—attributed to St. Teresa of Ávila

"We can't change the past, but we can be faithful in the present." I said this to one of the most unique audiences I have ever spoken to. Graceland Festival is one of the largest Christian festivals in the Netherlands. Its creative director, Rikko Voorberg, is one of the most fascinating Christian thought leaders I've ever met. "I just want people who have been hurt by the church to know that they can experience Jesus and find healing outside its walls, because Jesus is everywhere," Rikko told me in one of our first conversations.

I was at Graceland in August 2024 to speak on how to decolonize our faith in a way that prioritizes justice for our most marginalized neighbors. I was speaking to a predominantly white Dutch Christian audience—the descendants of Christians who supported colonization. And much like I do throughout this book, I was planning to gently point out how so much of our Western theological frameworks are colonized and must be decolonized so that we prioritize justice for all our marginalized neighbors, especially our neighbors suffering from violence and human trafficking.

The response to my talk was, fittingly, nothing but grace. Dozens of people thanked me for helping connect the dots and opening their eyes. Many even became monthly donors with a Dutch Christian justice organization in response to my talk. But I'll never forget Rikko's words to me, and I am thankful for his devotion to helping people hurt by the church to experience Jesus outside its walls. As I've shared before, if there's anything a decade of work in international human rights as a Christian has taught me, it's this: Jesus is on the margins, and he waits for us to join him in partnership there.

While it is indeed true that Christ has no body on earth but ours, Jesus doesn't *need* us to partner with him on the margins. As Jesus is Lord of all, if the church refuses to submit to his just ways (as seen throughout much of church history), Jesus is perfectly capable of achieving his purposes without the church. Still, he loves us and wants us to share in the liberating joy of the triune God who makes all things new. Jesus once told the Pharisees that if they tried to silence his disciples, then the rocks would cry out (Luke 19:40). For centuries, the Western church has had the opportunity to partner with Jesus on the margins, on the front lines of justice work. Instead, for so much of our history, we have often been the last to show up and the first to go away. I believe that because of our faithlessness in prioritizing justice in the Western church, God is awakening society and culture to prioritize justice. But as we've recently seen in the fight against racial injustice, society and culture are perfectly content to move on from justice issues when the political winds shift. We would do well to heed the words of St. Teresa of Ávila found at the opening of this chapter and allow God's compassion for the world to be shown through our works of love.

A church that resists the invitation of Jesus to partner with him in the work of justice is a church that is missing out on the deep joys of knowing and walking with him. If you're a Western Christian reading this book, you have actively benefited from the colonization of the Global South. And so have I. While I am a child of colonization, I am also a beneficiary of colonization. I became a beneficiary the day I moved to United States—and then to Canada after that. I too have benefited from the legacy of stolen wealth and stolen land. We cannot change the past, but we can be faithful in the present by partnering with Jesus in his work of justice for those people on the margins.

There are a few ways I think we can join Jesus on the margins as a Western church that has benefited from colonization.

Give

Growing up in the Global South church, I was raised to never let the offering basket pass by without contributing something. My parents would tithe their ten percent regularly *and* add cash on hand any time the offering basket went by. Other families would too. And on top of their own tithes and cash gifts, they would also give their children some money to put in the basket. Even today, if I attend church with my parents, who now live in rural South Carolina and attend their local Assemblies of God church, my parents will make sure I have some cash in hand for the basket when it passes by. This is never done out of obligation but always out of joy. If you're a Global South

Christian reading this, my guess is that you know exactly what I'm talking about.

This is why, when I first moved to the West, I was mortified to see scores of people let the offering basket pass by at church—entire rows at times. These days, most Western churches I have visited or preached at (both conservative and progressive) don't even pass offering baskets anymore. Some have stopped out of pastoral sensitivity to abusive theology centered around giving, but most just feel there is an awkwardness in talking about money from the pulpit.

As someone who has worked as a fundraiser at a human rights organization and who knows firsthand the power of money and its lack thereof in much of the Global South, I have zero hesitations when it comes to talking about money and generosity. In fact, one of my favorite things to do for pastor friends is to teach about money and generosity at their churches. There's a reason why Jesus himself taught so much about wealth and money: Money, when weaponized against our vulnerable neighbors, can be a force for evil. But money, when used redemptively, can also be a force for overwhelming good.

On our own, we can typically do little to effect systemic change with our finances. But when we pool our resources together, we can do some incredible things. A few years ago, the team I led challenged a few churches to ask for Christmas offerings to fund rescue operations (costing $10,000 CAD apiece) that would bring relief to children being sexually exploited online in the Philippines. The results were astounding. One Canadian church with just two hundred and fifty members (Talbot Street Christian Reformed Church in London, Ontario) raised nearly $100,000, exceeding their goal of $70,000. Another church with about a thousand members (Grandview Baptist Church in Kitchener, Ontario) raised $100,000, stretching well past their goal of $40,000. Compass Point Church in Burlington, Ontario (an eight-hundred-member church), doubled their goal of $40,000, raising $80,000. And Evangelical Free Church in Lethbridge, Alberta, tripled their goal of $100,000, raising $300,000 to fund the equivalent of thirty rescue operations!

None of these churches became generous justice-prioritizing churches overnight. Knowing the pastors well, I can tell you that it took years of intentional discipleship toward justice and generosity for these communities to get to this point. But once they did, it was beautiful to celebrate with them and watch them partake in the liberating joy of the triune God. By Christmas, the churches had raised over half a million dollars to fund the equivalent of fifty rescue operations in the Philippines.

Protest and Civil Disobedience

In October 2018, an Armenian refugee family was facing deportation from the Netherlands at the hands of the Dutch government. They had lived there for nine years before the highest court in the country ordered their deportation. Bethel Church, a Protestant congregation in The Hague, came to the aid of this family. After all legal efforts had failed, Bethel resorted to faithful protest. They sheltered the family on their church property and literally (physically) stood between the family and Dutch law enforcement. How did they do this? By taking advantage of a Dutch law that prohibits police from entering a church during a church service. In short, Bethel hosted a nonstop church service to protect the family while working to enact a policy that would allow the family to stay.

Soon, preachers and churchgoers from other Dutch churches showed up to keep the service going so that asylum-seeking children (just like this family's children) would be protected from deportation. My friend Ruben Vlot was one of many people who preached at this nonstop service of protest. Ruben says, "I strongly believe that the church has an essential role in our world. Without this connection, our faith risks becoming nothing more than a hollow theological concept, detached from the realities of life. Our Sunday worship of Jesus (who, by the way, was a refugee) should guide our actions and interactions throughout the week, influencing how we engage with all of creation."[1]

Word eventually spread throughout the European church. Soon church leaders across denominational lines and from neighboring countries like Germany, France, and Belgium also showed up to volunteer and preach. In the end, much of the Western European church rallied together to keep this church service going for ninety-six days—from October 2018 to January 2019—until the Dutch government changed its policies. That's a 2,300-hour church service, an astounding act of peaceful protest against a policy harming marginalized neighbors.

In the end, the Dutch church and much of the Western European church prompted government leaders in the Netherlands to open up the cases of several other refugee children and their families who were also seeking asylum and facing deportation. In a statement, church leaders said, "The Protestant Church of The Hague respects court orders but finds itself confronted with a dilemma: the choice between respecting the government and protecting the rights of a child."[2]

Now, when you hear the phrase "civil disobedience," your guardrails might go up. If I'm being honest, as an upper-middle-class Indian male now living a comfortable life in the West, my guard goes up too. This is probably because we have lived a life of privilege and comfort and have never needed to protest for any of our rights. But this is not the case for marginalized communities—including marginalized Christians. In fact, throughout global church history, from the early church to the civil rights movement in the United States and the anti-apartheid movement in South Africa, it has been normative for Christians on the margins to resort to peaceful, nonviolent protest and civil disobedience.

Dutch theologian Rozemarijn van't Einde has led numerous peaceful climate-action protests with other Dutch church leaders and everyday Christians. She writes,

> There is a strange myth in the Christian world that we have to be "nice." And by nice we mainly mean accommodating. We are not allowed to speak harsh words; that is not nice. We are not allowed to condemn bad practices; that is not nice. . . . The Bible is full of clear language condemning evil. Jesus used strong language and did not beat around the bush when addressing people who represented evil systems. For example, he used the term "brood of vipers" to expose the hypocrisy of the scribes, the orthodox teachers. Jesus was not naive about the destructive power of money and status.[3]

In a conversation I had with her, Rozemarijn told me, "We are called to be the salt of the earth, not the sugar of the earth." She's getting at a deep-seated theological tension many of us face: to be good citizens of empire *or* to peacefully protest the unjust laws of empire.

The early church faced this tension too as citizens of the Roman Empire. In Acts 4, we see Peter and John arrested and brought before the Sanhedrin (a Jewish religious tribunal sanctioned by the Roman Empire) because their holistic gospel activity has been causing a stir. When asked, "Under whose authority do you do this?" Peter and John basically go on to say they are acting on the authority of Jesus. They then have to explain who Jesus is and how he has already been rejected by the Roman Empire. When the religious and political authorities instruct the apostles to cease their gospel proclamation, they tell them, "Sorry, but we're answerable to a higher authority," before going on their way and continuing the work of gospel proclamation (both in word and deed). This in turn leads to a revival of the Holy Spirit and mutual love and economic equality among the members of the early church in Jerusalem.

Church leaders like Augustine, Thomas Aquinas, John Calvin, Dietrich Bonhoeffer, and Martin Luther King Jr. have disagreed on some theological matters, but much like the Dutch church and my friend Rozemarijn, one thing they have all agreed on is this: When we the church are asked to choose between our allegiance to empire and our allegiance to Jesus, we must always choose our allegiance to Jesus and his just gospel, regardless of the cost.

Vision Trips

If you've grown up in the Western church, you're probably familiar with the concept of mission trips. If you're passionate about justice and are asking questions about decolonization, you likely also have mixed feelings about mission trips, especially short-term mission trips.

Mission trips can have good qualities. For example, Western Christians are exposed to the church in the Global South and are given firsthand opportunities to build relationships with Christians there. Global South Christians are then able to connect with Western Christians and establish funding partnerships. That said, many Global South leaders and missiologists have argued that the current mission trip model of the Western church is harmful for our Global South neighbors.[4] Generally speaking, short-term mission trips can have the possibility of being transactional, dehumanizing, and extractive of our Global South neighbors. This is the case when their poverty is commodified and the savior complex of Western Christians is glorified. How do we redeem mission trips in a way that is decolonized, collaborative, and justice oriented? Instead of reinventing the wheel, I'd like to propose a decolonized trip model that many Christian humanitarian organizations in the West already leverage.

"Vision trips" are fundamentally different from "mission trips." While both can be brief, mission trips have historically been opportunities to "go and do." Vision trips, on the other hand, are opportunities to "come and see what God is already doing." Or to put it in another way, mission trips are fundamentally about "going and doing," whereas vision trips are for "going, seeing, and learning."

Vision trips require immense humility and patience on the part of Western Christians. They don't offer the gratification of building homes or painting buildings and patting ourselves on the back at the end of the trip (not that there isn't a need for building homes or painting buildings). Vision trips require us to humble ourselves, to sit at the feet of our Global South siblings in Christ, and to ask questions with a posture of curiosity. They require us to put aside our ingrained disposition to assume the posture of a knowledgeable teacher and to ask local leaders questions like the following:

Can you tell me about the history and culture(s) of your region?
What are your greatest obstacles in doing justice work?
What are your greatest joys in the work of justice?
How can Western Christian communities like mine come alongside your community in this work of justice?
Who else should I be connecting with and learning from?

Given my context in global human rights work, I'm obviously sharing these thoughts from a global perspective. But the same type of trip can be done with local and national justice partners in and around your faith community's urban, suburban, and rural geographic region. Vision trips can be an excellent way to expose your community to justice issues locally and globally, in addition to giving it an opportunity to build relationships of mutuality instead of hierarchy. So instead of thinking *What can we do to fix this?* we approach new situations with the question *How can we learn and be shaped as we partner together in God's kingdom?*

A fruitful vision trip starts with a day or two of historical and cultural immersion, when attendees tour the area to get a better understanding of the people, history, and culture. Then attendees can spend time meeting with local experts to learn more about the scope of the challenges their communities face, finding out about current efforts that are already underway, how local Christians are already partnering to end injustices, and what resource gaps exist that keep the work from moving forward. Throughout this trip, attendees can also get to know the local culture by immersing themselves in the languages and partaking of local foods that the communities they seek to serve are proud of. Living incarnationally (just like Jesus and his apostles did) can be tremendously helpful.

The most important part of a vision trip comes after participants return home. Vision trips are intended to inspire you and your community to cast a fresh vision for how you can come alongside the work already taking place (instead of creating your own initiative and expecting local communities to meet your preferences as the funding partner). Local leaders in the Global South, especially local Christian leaders, will always have the best sense of the solutions needed to tackle the justice issues their communities face. It is thus of utmost importance to us as Western church leaders to trust and empower them to solve these problems in the ways they deem best. Now, this is not to say that we shouldn't have checks and balances; every donor and partner deserves to know exactly what their funds are going toward. A decolonized way of partnering in justice must, however, rely on local leaders to determine priorities and strategies—as opposed to leaders in foreign, corporate boardrooms deciding local priorities and strategies while intentionally or unintentionally weaponizing funding as a means of control.

Additionally, a decolonized way of forming financial partnerships is to ensure that ministry workers are compensated well, in ways that are commensurate with industry salary and benefit ranges and level of skill or experience. It is critical that we get this part right as Christians because we cannot have any credibility with people on the margins or with people outside the church if we expect our partners and justice workers to do their work while treating them poorly in the name of Christ.

I owe so much of my own spiritual formation as a justice advocacy leader to vision trips that I've participated in or led these past many years. I attended my first such trip as a seventeen-year-old campus-ministry leader with the Union of Evangelical Students in India, which is the Indian affiliate of the International Fellowship of Evangelical Students (IFES). I was sent as a delegate to Singapore's national Fellowship of Evangelical Students (FES) conference to observe how they did campus ministry and to return back with observations and recommendations. One of my biggest takeaways from that trip was the FES's heart for migrant workers in Singapore (one of the richest countries in Asia), who were often exploited through unjust employment practices. For context, this was right after the Third Lausanne Congress on World Evangelization published the Cape Town Commitment, a global evangelical church commitment to double-down on social justice as an expression of the gospel of Jesus of Nazareth. And this passion for justice was now being fanned into flame by evangelical leaders in Singapore. I came back from this conference asking why the IFES movement in India (of which I was a leader) was not contextualizing the gospel for the work of justice as much as our Singaporean siblings were, especially given our context's many justice needs. This experience shaped me even as I later served as a student leader with InterVarsity Christian Fellowship at Georgia State University.

As someone who has led multiple vision trips, I have seen firsthand how they've deeply shaped Western Christians to champion the marginalized communities they've learned from and to mobilize countless others to pray, advocate, and partner on their behalf.

Justice work is always more effective and joy filled when done in community. Partnerships are an exciting way to go about this work. Nevertheless, building effective partnerships takes effort, foresight, and resourcing over the long haul. One of the most significant (and underrated) ways Western Christians can partner with Christians on the margins (especially in the Global South) is through our resources. We can't change the past, and we can't change the ways we've benefited from colonization and slavery, but we can be faithful in the present with the bounty that we find ourselves entrusted with.

Another way to partner with Jesus and marginalized communities in the work of justice is through protest, more specifically (since we're all about seeking justice Jesus's way), peaceful protests. This way of partnering with marginalized communities is probably one that you find yourself unfamiliar or uncomfortable with. But there's precedent for this form of protest, which is normative throughout global church history.

Vision trips are also an effective, decolonized way to faithfully partner with marginalized communities. These trips allow Western Christians to embody a posture of curiosity and humility by learning firsthand from marginalized communities and Christians on the margins. Participants then return home and prayerfully cast fresh vision for how they can partner with the marginalized communities they have spent time observing and learning from.

REFLECTION QUESTIONS

1. How can you spend more time becoming a student of justice issues facing marginalized communities locally and globally?
2. Who are some trusted individual or organizational voices you can learn from as you seek to cultivate curiosity about justice issues affecting marginalized communities?
3. What "red flags" would you watch out for regarding justice organizations and leaders you would like to partner with?
4. Can you identify one or two trusted friends you can process justice-related partnership opportunities with?

AFTERWORD

> In the Church of Sant'Egidio in Rome, home of an extraordinary community of laypeople devoted to working for the poor, there is an old crucifix that portrays Christ without arms. When I asked about its importance to the community, I was told that it shows how God relies on us to do God's work in the world.
>
> —Archbishop Desmond Tutu, *God Is Not a Christian: And Other Provocations*

I write this concluding section a few days after the 2024 US presidential election. Over the past decade, there has been plenty of conjecture about how we have arrived at such a divisive, fear-driven, and pessimistic place. Concurrently, I have also noticed very little hopeful vision-casting by voices within and outside the church for a way forward. While this book offers a certain degree of diagnosis on why, generally speaking, justice is not the natural disposition of the Western church, I have attempted to use these pages to offer a positive vision for a hope-filled way forward.

Throughout the book, I have made a conscious effort to amplify voices from the margins and the Global South church that we are not likely accustomed to hearing from: Black liberation theologians, feminist theologians, Catholic clergy, St. Thomas Indian / Mar Thoma leaders, etc. In fact, most of the sources I cite in this book are by people who I was taught to distrust and look down on as a Western Christian. That's probably because these voices challenge our safe theological bubbles. But this is also likely because these voices challenge the Western, empire-shaped power structures of the postcolonial world we live in. My prayer is that these voices from the margins will shape us and challenge our neatly packed Western ideas—just like they have challenged mine. And my hope is that we will all end up with a more beautiful, ancient, Jesus-centered, and justice-oriented faith.

I try to prioritize these teachers because reclaiming the justice of Jesus in our churches today means sitting at the feet of our siblings in Christ who have a perspective of him that is different from our own. These prophetic voices on the margins are without a doubt the best teachers on how to resist the oppressive ways of empires while loving God and neighbor faithfully.

If you grew up in the evangelical church, you are probably familiar with Jeremiah 29:11: "For surely I know the plans I have for you, says the Lord, plans for your welfare and not for harm, to give you a future with hope." Perhaps you've seen this verse on a bumper sticker or a refrigerator magnet. Or maybe someone has written this for you on a greeting card. The words of this verse are beautiful and inspiring. But if we delve into the context of this verse, we will see that it was not written to recent graduates or those moving cross-country for a job opportunity, it was written to an exiled Jewish community living in captivity under a colonizing empire.

Empires use their power to extract labor, wealth, and resources from those under their dominion—but especially their colonized, foreign subjects. Empires are not designed to care about human flourishing; they're designed to care only about the flourishing of a few powerful ruling elites and those who serve their interests. And the Jewish people in captivity were not among the ruling elite of the Babylonian Empire.

Just as many Western Christians may find themselves dismayed by the realities of the church's historical participation in the oppression of our marginalized neighbors, the Jewish people in exile found themselves distraught, trampled on, and without hope. It is in this context that the prophet Jeremiah declares prophetic hope for the Jewish exiles through a rich exhortation: "Thus says the LORD of hosts, the God of Israel, to all the exiles whom I have sent into exile from Jerusalem to Babylon: Build houses and live in them; plant gardens and eat what they produce" (Jer. 29:4–5).

Did you catch that? Instead of instructing the people of God to resist the oppressive ways of empire with violence, despair, or cynicism, Jeremiah tells the people living in exile to resist by building houses, planting gardens, and eating healthy food. Jeremiah goes on to exhort God's people in exile: "But seek the welfare of the city where I have sent you into exile, and pray to the LORD on its behalf, for in its welfare you will find your welfare" (Jer. 29:7).

I want us to hone in on the word "welfare"; this word shows up later in Jeremiah 29:11 as well. The word "welfare" in North America can have a negative connotation, with many Christians associating it with government handouts. But this is a very narrow interpretation. For a more accurate understanding of welfare, we need to go back to the original Hebrew in Jeremiah 29:11: shalom. Shalom means something much deeper than welfare; shalom means *wholeness*. And wholeness for many of our poor and oppressed neighbors demands their (peaceful) liberation from the unjust power structures restricting their human flourishing.

Those of us who have the privilege of living in North America find ourselves either within or close to one of the most powerful empires in the history of humankind: the American Empire. Throughout the Bible, we see the people of God living in faithful resistance to the unjust ways of a wide variety of empires (regardless of who was emperor or caesar within these empires). For example, Jeremiah was written within the context of the Babylonian Empire. And Jesus teaches the Beatitudes to a Jewish people oppressed by the Roman Empire. The people of God were always meant to be distinctive from such power structures so that we can be faithful by caring for those on the margins and doing the work of peacemaking.

The God of the oppressed sees the people who are used up and cast aside by empires. God knows their pain, hears their cries, and tells them to build houses, plant gardens, eat well, be fruitful and multiply. And he tells them to seek the shalom of their city—because in its shalom, we will find our shalom. This is also what faithfulness as followers of Jesus looks like: advancing the flourishing of life by building houses, planting gardens, and eating organic, farm-to-table food.

Historically, we see that empires thrive on creating and fostering environments of fear. But fear chokes our imagination and makes us respond in foolish ways. And like the colonizer's gospel, fear divides us to conquer. In a climate of fear, let us embody the justice of Jesus in a way that unites to heal. Let us seek ecumenical unity within the church and pluralistic unity outside the church so that we can present a countercultural vision to a divided society. Let us obey the biblical exhortation to "fear not" while exploring and imagining ancient and new ways to find shalom in our world today.

May we be liberated from fear and despair as we actively choose hope, courage, and conviction in the days to come: regardless of what this may cost us.

ACKNOWLEDGMENTS

It takes a village to write a book. This book is indeed a community effort.

The first group of people I'd like to acknowledge are the people who challenged me to dig deep into exploring a Christian theology that actually sounds like good news for people in poverty and oppression. To all the survivors of violence and abuse who have patiently taught me over the years: I continue to be inspired and amazed by your resilience.

The next group I would like to thank are those who I've had the privilege to co-labor in the work of justice alongside over the past decade—from the Philippines and South Asia to Bolivia and the Netherlands and beyond. This book would not exist without you patiently teaching me how to pursue justice in an ecumenical, Jesus-centered way. To my longtime mentor in this work of justice, Anu George Canjanathoppil: Thank you for supporting me and greatly encouraging me in this journey of writing a book that I hope will be a gift to the global church.

This book would also not exist without my literary agent, Morgan Strehlow, and the team at The Bindery. Thank you for seeing the raw potential in my voice, talking me into submitting

Acknowledgments

a book proposal, and guiding me every step of the way as a new author! Katelyn Beaty and the whole Brazos team, thank you for believing in this project and for all your wise input and guidance along the way as well.

I'm also grateful for the support and care of my personal community here in North America: my parents, Praveen and Susan Thomas; my sister, Hannah Thomas; and my close circle of friends. Brian and Neftaly Garcia, Marc and Tryphena Perumalla Gagnon, Steve and Robyn Elliott, James Sholl and Emily Sherk, Timo and Siobhan Koch: Thank you for sitting with me in my highest of highs and lowest of lows. Phil Calvert, thank you for being the first person to encourage me to write a book and cast a vision for how it might benefit the church. Krista Bowman, thank you for being such an encouraging intellectual partner with your brilliant scholarship and deep spiritual wisdom. To my close companion, my goldendoodle Georgia, thank you for embodying the faithful and loyal presence of Jesus to me every day.

To my spiritual and ecclesial communities, Champion Life Centre, Lakeside Church, and the Diocese of St. Anthony: Thank you for allowing me to keep hope alive in my heart for the Western church! To the Canadian church: Thank you for embodying a healthy vision for what a justice-centered Western church on the margins can look like. My Canadian clergy friends—Jeremy Johnson, Paul Berenguer, Robyn Elliott James Sholl, Scott Lanigan, Marc Gagnon, Christine Woods, Jeremy Duncan, Jonathan David Smith, Jessica Collins, James Paton, and Phil Reinders—deserve special mention.

And last but by no means least, thank you to my dear friend Rev. Dr. David Harvey. You have been one of the most profound theological and missional influences in my life, and much of this book is a result of our conversations in close friendship over the past few years.

NOTES

Chapter 1 Why Justice Seems Antithetical to the Western Church

1. "Message to the Christian Churches," posted by Jordan B Peterson, YouTube, July 12, 2022, 10 min., 50 sec., https://www.youtube.com/watch?v=e7ytLpO7mj0.

2. Martin Luther King Jr., "Remaining Awake Through the Great Revolution," speech delivered at the National Cathedral, Washington, DC, March 31, 1968.

3. Walter D. Mignolo and Catherine E. Walsh, *On Decoloniality: Concepts, Analytics, Praxis* (Duke University Press, 2018), 115.

4. Sarah Trembath, "History of Colonization," Antiracist Praxis, American University, accessed December 20, 2024, https://subjectguides.library.american.edu/c.php?g=1025915&p=7749710.

5. Willie James Jennings, *A Christian Imagination: Theology and the Origins of Race* (Yale University Press, 2011).

6. Jemar Tisby, "The Curse of Ham and Biblical Justifications for Slavery," *Zondervan Academic* (Blog), February 11, 2022, https://zondervanacademic.com/blog/the-curse-of-ham-and-biblical-justifications-for-slavery.

7. In support of this argument, see Leo G. Perdue, *Israel and Empire: A Postcolonial History of Israel and Early Judaism* (T&T Clark, 2015), 277.

8. Richard Twiss, *Rescuing the Gospel from Cowboys: A Native American Expression of the Jesus Way* (InterVarsity, 2015), 28–41.

9. Joseph Daniel, *Ecumenism in Praxis: A Historical Critique of the Malankara Mar Thoma Syrian Church*, Studies in the Intercultural History of Christianity 159 (Peter Lang, 2014), 68–69.

10. Daniel, *Ecumenism in Praxis*, 68–69.

11. Zach Lambert (@ZachWLambert), "The vast majority of the people," X (formerly Twitter), March 22, 2022, https://x.com/ZachWLambert/status/1506311869975478284.

Chapter 2 The Cost of Just Discipleship

1. Dietrich Bonhoeffer, *The Cost of Discipleship*, trans. R. H. Fuller (Touchstone, 1995), 42.

2. Timothy Dalrymple, "Abuse in the Church and the Road to Jericho," *Christianity Today*, June 3, 2022, https://www.christianitytoday.com/2022/06/sexual-abuse-victims-good-samaritan/.

3. Martin Luther King Jr., "A Time to Break the Silence," in *A Testament of Hope: The Essential Writings and Speeches of Martin Luther King, Jr.*, ed. James M. Washington (HarperOne, 2003), 241.

4. Nathan Dirks, email to author, March 28, 2024.

5. Matthew Murphy, email to author, March 24, 2024.

6. Cameron Bellm, "St. Óscar Romero," in *The Modern Saints: Portraits and Reflections on the Saints*, ed. Gracie Morbitzer (Convergent Books, 2023), 67.

7. Nicole Winfield, "Romero Controversial in Death Too," *Lakeland Ledger*, August 4, 2007, https://www.theledger.com/story/news/2007/08/04/romero-controversial-in-death-too/25822537007/.

8. Sarah Bessey, *Field Notes for the Wilderness: Practices for an Evolving Faith* (Convergent Books, 2024), 67.

9. Walter Brueggemann, *The Prophetic Imagination*, 40th anniv. ed. (Fortress, 2018), 3.

Chapter 3 How Churches Today Are Prioritizing Justice

1. Jill Lawless, "Church of England Sheds Light on 'Shameful' Slave Trade Ties," AP News, January 31, 2023, https://apnews.com/article/anglicanism-religion-dd656463d44d6348750d57cc6c91c0c7.

2. Rachel Russell, "Church of England Announces £100m Fund After Slavery Links," BBC, January 10, 2023, https://www.bbc.com/news/uk-64228673.

3. Lawless, "Church of England."

4. Russell, "Church of England."

5. Francis Martin, "Open Letters Exchanged as Save the Parish Questions Commissioners' Slavery-Legacy Grants," *Church Times*, January 16, 2023, https://www.churchtimes.co.uk/articles/2023/20-january/news/uk/open-letters-exchanged-as-save-the-parish-questions-commissioners-slavery-legacy-grants.

6. Jemar Tisby, *The Color of Compromise: The Truth About the American Church's Complicity in Racism*, (Zondervan, 2020), 52.

Chapter 4 Decolonizing Our Theology

1. Rafiq Khoury, "The Conflict of Narratives: From Memory to Prophecy," in *The Invention of History: A Century of Interplay Between Theology and Politics in Palestine*, ed. Mitri Raheb (Diyar, 2011), 266.

2. Mitri Raheb, *Faith in the Face of Empire: The Bible Through Palestinian Eyes* (Orbis Books, 2014), 21.

3. Howard Thurman, *Jesus and the Disinherited* (1949; repr., Beacon, 1996), 19.

4. Peter Schuurman, "A Train Wreck in Slow Motion: Review of the Podcast *The Rise and Fall of Mars Hill* by Mike Cosper," *Christian Courier*, October 27, 2021, https://www.christiancourier.ca/a-train-wreck-in-slow-motion/.

5. Rachel Held Evans, *Searching for Sunday: Loving, Leaving, and Finding the Church* (Nelson Books, 2015), xvi.
6. Anthony G. Reddie, "Dealing with the Two Deadly Ds: Deconstructing Whiteness and Decolonizing the Curriculum of Theological Education," in *Deconstructing Whiteness, Empire and Mission*, ed. Anthony G. Reddie and Carol Troupe (SCM, 2023), 54.
7. Reddie, "Dealing with the Two Deadly Ds," 55–57.
8. Eve Parker, "Re-Distributing Theological Knowledge in Theological Education as an Act of Distributive Justice in Contemporary Christian Mission," in Reddie and Troupe, *Deconstructing Whiteness, Empire and Mission*, 41.
9. Parker, "Re-Distributing Theological Knowledge," 48.
10. Reddie, "Dealing with the Two Deadly Ds," 55.
11. Reddie, "Dealing with the Two Deadly Ds," 57.
12. Reddie, "Dealing with the Two Deadly Ds," 53.

Chapter 5 Decolonizing Our Communities

1. Chandra Mallampalli, *South Asia's Christians: Between Hindu and Muslim* (Oxford University Press, 2023), 31–33.
2. Mitri Raheb, *The Politics of Persecution: Middle Eastern Christians in an Age of Empire* (Baylor University Press, 2021), 42.
3. Raheb, *Politics of Persecution*, 38.
4. Lakeside Church, "Our Statement on Belief and Practice," accessed February 21, 2025, https://thechurchco-production.s3.amazonaws.com/uploads/sites/8992/2024/08/Statement-on-Belief-and-Practice-Lakeside-Church.pdf.
5. Joseph Daniel, *Ecumenism in Praxis: A Historical Critique of the Malankara Mar Thoma Syrian Church*, Studies in the Intercultural History of Christianity 159 (Peter Lang, 2014), 51.
6. Daniel, *Ecumenism in Praxis*, 51.
7. Raheb, *Politics of Persecution*, 38.
8. Paul D. Miller, "What Is Christian Nationalism?," *Christianity Today*, February 3, 2021, https://www.christianitytoday.com/ct/2021/february-web-only/what-is-christian-nationalism.html.
9. Lisa Sharon Harper, foreword to *If God Still Breathes, Why Can't I? Black Lives Matter and Biblical Authority*, by Angela N. Parker (Eerdmans, 2021), 10.
10. See Mallory Moench, "Bethlehem Reverend Delivers 'Christ in the Rubble' Christmas Sermon amid Gaza Conflict," *Time*, December 24, 2023, https://time.com/6550851/bethlehem-christmas-sermon-nativity-rubble/.
11. Daniel, *Ecumenism in Praxis*, 59.
12. Daniel, *Ecumenism in Praxis*, 60.
13. Daniel, *Ecumenism in Praxis*, 76–81.
14. Daniel, *Ecumenism in Praxis*, 83.
15. Daniel, *Ecumenism in Praxis*, 85.
16. Peniel Rajkumar, "Postcolonialism and Re-Stor(y)ing," in *Deconstructing Whiteness, Empire and Mission*, ed. Anthony G. Reddie and Carol Troupe (SCM, 2023), 113.

Chapter 6 Decolonizing Our Budgets

1. Joseph Daniel, *Ecumenism in Praxis: A Historical Critique of the Malankara Mar Thoma Syrian Church*, Studies in the Intercultural History of Christianity 159 (Peter Lang, 2014), 80.

2. Daniel, *Ecumenism in Praxis*, 84.

3. Citizens for Public Justice and International Justice Mission Canada, "A Call to Strengthen Canada's Protection to Central American Survivors of Gender-Based Violence," Citizens for Public Justice, December 12, 2022, https://cpj.ca/report/a-call-to-strengthen-canadas-protection-to-central-american-survivors-of-gender-based-violence/.

Chapter 7 Prayer

1. Desmond Brown, "This Kitchener, Ont., Church Uses Portion of Its Budget for Indigenous Reparations for 'Harm Done,'" CBC News, September 29, 2024, https://www.cbc.ca/news/canada/kitchener-waterloo/indigenous-reparations-kitchener-stirling-mennonite-church-1.7333661.

2. Douglas E. Oakman, *Jesus and the Peasants* (Cascade Books, 2008), 70.

3. Joerg Rieger, "Liberative Theologies of Poverty and Class," in *Introducing Liberative Theologies*, ed. Miguel A. De La Torre (Orbis Books, 2015), 153.

Chapter 8 Advocacy

1. Jemar Tisby, *The Color of Compromise: The Truth About the American Church's Complicity in Racism* (Zondervan, 2020), 99.

2. Bassem Mroue and Kareem Chehayebap, "Investigation into Beirut's Massive 2020 Port Blast Resumes," AP News, January 23, 2023, https://apnews.com/article/politics-beirut-lebanon-03eb5ff04f6ad86b3d0d6fb2ab25bdd6.

3. Marwan Aboul-Zelof, "Despair and Light from the Rubble of Beirut," Gospel Coalition, August 5, 2020, https://www.thegospelcoalition.org/article/despair-light-rubble-beirut/.

4. Nikayla Reize, "Physician Heal Thyself," Nikayla's Substack, August 7, 2024, https://nikaylareize.substack.com/p/physician-heal-thyself.

Chapter 9 Partnership

1. Ruben Vlot, email message to author, August 31, 2024.

2. Francesca Paris, "Months-Long Dutch Church Service to Protect Migrants Ends After Policy Shift," NPR, January 31, 2019, https://www.npr.org/2019/01/31/690403074/months-long-dutch-church-service-to-protect-migrants-ends-after-policy-shift.

3. Rozemarijn van't Einde, *Rebelleren Voor Het Leven: Een Dominee In Actie Voor Klimaatrechtvaardigheid* (Kokboekencentrum, 2023). The author provided an English translation for me.

4. See, e.g., Mekdes Haddis, *A Just Mission: Laying Down Power and Embracing Mutuality* (InterVarsity, 2022).

JOASH P. THOMAS

Rev. Joash P. Thomas is a public theologian and acclaimed international speaker. Born and raised in India, he ran a political consulting and lobbying firm in the United States before working as an international human rights leader. He is an ordained minister in the Diocese of St. Anthony in the Communion of Evangelical Episcopal Churches and lives in a multiethnic community in Hamilton, Ontario (Canada).

CONNECT WITH JOASH

- joashpthomas.com
- Joash Thomas
- @JoashPThomas
- @JoashPThomas
- @JoashPThomas
- @JoashPThomas
- @JoashPThomas